SEGREGATION LIVES
DEMOCRACY DIES

JKAC

OKLAHOMA STANDS FOR
FREEDOM
EQUALITY
JUSTICE

MAY 1 - 2018

D1468793

THE LIFE OF
JIMMY
STEWART

A PASSION FOR
EQUALITY

THE LIFE OF
JIMMY
STEWART

**BY VICKI MILES-LAGRANGE
AND BOB BURKE**

FOREWORD BY ANDREW YOUNG

KENNY A. FRANKS
SERIES EDITOR

GINI MOORE CAMPBELL
ASSOCIATE EDITOR

OKLAHOMA HERITAGE ASSOCIATION
OKLAHOMA *TRACKMAKER* SERIES

OTHER BOOKS

BY BOB BURKE:

Lyle Boren: Rebel Congressman
3,500 Years of Burkes
These Be Thine Arms Forever
The Stories and Speeches of Lyle H. Boren
Corn, Cattle, and Moonshine:
  A History of Hochatown, Oklahoma
Like a Prairie Fire
Push Back the Darkness
The Irish Connection
Lyle H. Boren: The Eloquent Congressman
Dewey F. Bartlett: The Bartlett Legacy
Glen D. Johnson, Sr.: The Road to Washington
An American Jurist:
  The Life of Alfred P. Murrah
Mike Monroney: Oklahoma Liberal
Roscoe Dunjee: Champion of Civil Rights
From Oklahoma to Eternity:
  The Life of Wiley Post and the Winnie Mae
Out From the Shadows: The Life of John J. Harden

Copyright ©1999

by Oklahoma Heritage Association

All rights reserved. No part of this book may be
reproduced or utilized in any form or by any
means, electronic or mechanical, including
photocopying and recording, or by any
information storage and retrieval system, without
permission from the copyright holders.

Printed in the United States of America

ISBN 1-885596-12-x

LC Number 99-70170

Designed by Carol Haralson

OKLAHOMA HERITAGE ASSOCIATION

201 NORTHWEST FOURTEENTH STREET

OKLAHOMA CITY, OKLAHOMA 73103

OKLAHOMA HERITAGE

ASSOCIATION PUBLICATIONS

COMMITTEE 1999

Everett E. Berry, *Chairman, Stillwater*
W. R. " Dick" Stubbs, *Vice Chairman, Henryetta*
Sharon Bell, *Tulsa*
Mrs. Everett Berry, *Stillwater*
James H. Boren, *Tahlequah*
Edwin C. Boynton, *Durant*
Bob Burke, *Oklahoma City*
Don Ferrell, *Chandler*
LeRoy H. Fischer, *Stillwater*
Fred C. Harlan, *Okmulgee*
John Hefner, *Oklahoma City*
Virginia Kidd, *Poteau*
Vicki Miles-LaGrange, *Oklahoma City*
B. Chesley Montague, *Lawton*
G. Lee Stidham, *Ex-Officio, Checotah*
Ann Woolley, *Ada*
Waldo Zerger, *Tulsa*

Page two: Parades through the streets of
downtown Oklahoma City in the early 1960s
drew attention to the growing sentiment of
support for civil rights for all races. (Courtesy
The Daily Oklahoman.)

Page six: Pickets leave Calvary Baptist Church
headed for downtown to draw attention to the
economic boycott of businesses who refused to
serve blacks. (Courtesy *The Daily Oklahoman.*)

Page four: Jimmy Stewart.

Page ten: A focus of the early sit-down
demonstrations at Oklahoma City eating
establishments was the lunch counter at the John
A. Brown Department Store. (Courtesy *The
Daily Oklahoman.*)

DEDICATED TO THE MEN AND WOMEN

OF OKLAHOMA NATURAL GAS COMPANY

FOR 92 YEARS

OF EXEMPLARY SERVICE TO OKLAHOMA,

AND TO THE ONEOK FOUNDATION INC.,

FOR MAKING THE PUBLICATION

OF THIS BOOK POSSIBLE.

OKLAHOMA
NATURAL
GAS
A DIVISION OF ONEOK

Contents

Foreword

Judge Vicki Miles-LaGrange and Bob Burke have written a book about a powerful player in the movement toward change in this United States. In this book, the life of Jimmy Stewart is chronicled in detail as he strived, even in childhood, to combat racism and poverty. The book meticulously describes Mr. Stewart's incredible rise from janitor to assistant to the vice president of one of his state's most powerful utilities.

In 1968, Dr. Martin Luther King, Jr. warned us that our nation could not survive with "islands of poverty in the midst of an ocean of material wealth." Like slavery, poverty is an abomination. It is intolerable.

The life of Jimmy Stewart serves as a positive role model for people around the globe who no longer find poverty acceptable.

Andrew Young
Atlanta, Georgia
August 13, 1998

Andrew Young was a top aide to Dr. Martin Luther King, Jr. during the civil rights movement. He later served three terms in the United States House of Representatives from Georgia's Fifth District. President Jimmy Carter named him United States Ambassador to the United Nations in 1977. An ordained minister, human rights activist, author, and international businessman, Young served two terms as mayor of Atlanta and was co-chairman of the Centennial Olympic Games in Atlanta in 1996.

Acknowledgments

The authors acknowledge the help of many people who helped transform an overwhelming research project into a comprehensive story of a great man's life. We are grateful to: Don Sherry, Oklahoma Natural Gas Company Communications Manager, and retired ONG executives Charles C. Ingram, Max Knotts, and William N. "Bill" Pirtle for providing historical material and personal recollections of Jimmy Stewart's long association with the company; Denyvetta Davis, manager of the Ralph Ellison Library, and her assistant Laurin Linscott, who always have a smile and a helping hand for researchers; Carol Campbell, Melissa Hayer, Mary Phillips, and Robin Davison at *The Daily Oklahoman* archives and information center for providing invaluable photos of Stewart's life; Stewart's children, Don, James Jr., and Zandra, daughter-in-law Eleanor, and granddaughter Donna Lewis for sharing intimate stories of their father and grandfather; Stewart's widow Mae Lois, though frail in body, and granddaughter Jeania Alexander, for making us feel welcome in their home to search through stacks of files and photographs; Bervis McBride Jr., Stewart's nephew and terrific source of family history and photographs; Eric Dabney and Debi Engles for research and computer support; Bill Welge, Rodger Harris, and Judith Michener at the Oklahoma Historical Society, always gracious in opening up their incredible oral history collection; Oklahoma Heritage Association President Lee Allan Smith and Executive Director Dr. Paul Lambert for their unfailing support of the preservation of Oklahoma history; the publishing world's greatest editors, Dr. Kenny Franks and Gini Moore Campbell; and Carol Haralson, America's best book designer;

And to Russell Perry, Hannah Atkins, Judge Jerry Salyer, Reverend W.K. Jackson, Bill Pirtle, Don Sherry, Don Stewart, James Stewart, Jr., Zandra Stewart, Denyvetta Davis and Eric Dabney for reviewing the manuscript for accuracy and direction of content.

Vicki Miles-LaGrange and Bob Burke

Jimmy, at age 12, in 1924.

ONE
HARD TIMES

TEARS TRICKLED DOWN the face of the eight-year-old boy as he stood at the side of his father's casket. "How could this happen? How could God take Daddy?" the boy asked his mother.

It was October, 1920, on Peach Street in Oklahoma City. With his father's passing, young Jimmy Stewart was left with only his mother and older half-sister Johnnie to care for him and his brothers and sisters.

Maggie Stewart patted her son on the head as she wondered aloud, "Dear God, how will we ever make it?" Big sister Johnnie, 17 years old, earned a few dollars a week as a beauty shop maid. She comforted her mother, "Mama, I'll work hard. Jimmy can work hard too. I know we'll be all right."

For the next few years Maggie and her family came to know the painful meaning of real poverty.

James Edward Stewart was born September 16, 1912, in Plano, Collin County, Texas to Zena Thomas Stewart, born in Mississippi in 1875, and Mary Magdeline "Maggie" Fegalee Stewart, born in Freestone County, Texas, June 9, 1882. James, or "Jimmy," as he was affectionately known later in life, was the third child of the Zena and Maggie Stewart union. Zena Thomas Stewart, Jr. was born May 26, 1908, and Essie Berta Stewart was born July 13, 1910.

The elder Stewart worked as a common laborer in a cottonseed oil mill and preached on weekends in any Baptist church whose

Zena Thomas Stewart, Jimmy's father, was born in Mississippi in 1875. He moved to Texas to raise his family and preach on weekends in local Baptist churches.

Mary Magdaline Fegalee Stewart, Jimmy's mother, was called "Maggie" by her friends and family. She was born in Texas in 1882. She died in Wichita, Kansas, December 26, 1961.

Jimmy, center, as a baby. On the left is Zena Thomas Stewart, Jr., born in 1908 and Essie Berta Stewart born in 1910.

parishioners would listen to his gospel message. There were plenty of mouths to feed in the Stewart household. Reverend Stewart had two children, Alfred and Lona Mae, from a previous marriage. Maggie also had two girls, Ella and Johnnie.

In 1916 Reverend Stewart found work in Oklahoma City and soon sent for his growing family. He was 47 years old when malaria attacked his body in 1920 and took him from his wife and children. He died in the family's two-room bungalow on Peach Street.

After her husband's death, Maggie took her new role as the head of the Stewart family seriously. She took in laundry, earning just 35 cents a day. Johnnie supplemented the family income by taking odd cleaning jobs and serving food at local cafes.

Hard times forced Jimmy to grow up prematurely. Part of his learning had to do with survival. He roamed the alley picking up rags, bottles, copper, and iron to sell at junk yards. He shined shoes, washed dishes, and made deliveries for a neighborhood drug

Maggie Stewart (seated) with her children in the 1940s. Left to right: Johnnie, Z.T., Jr., Essie, Jimmy, Ella.

store. Jimmy was now the man of the house, at age eight, since his older brother and sisters had left home or gone to live with relatives.

In the winters Jimmy and Johnnie kept the fire going in their small frame house by walking along the railroad tracks next to the Creek Coal Company to gather chunks of coal that had fallen out of bins.

The Stewarts lived in West Town, one of the villages settled by black families along the North Canadian River near present downtown Oklahoma City. Housing conditions were primitive in West Town, Sand Town, Walnut Grove, and South Town in 1921. Five years earlier, in 1916, the City Council of Oklahoma City passed an ordinance that made it a crime for blacks to build churches, schools, or community buildings in any ward of the city that was at least 75 percent white.[1]

The ordinance was an overt attempt to keep blacks in the small, overcrowded section just east, west, and south of downtown. There was no room for expansion as more black families moved into the area. Every attempt made by blacks to break out of their ghetto was met with disappointment, arrest, and even bombings. The home of Beulah Maxwell, a black hairdresser who moved into a white neighborhood, was destroyed by a bomb in 1919.[2]

One Oklahoma City newspaper endorsed the idea of keeping blacks confined to the villages along the river. Harlow's Weekly editorialized, "Segregation benefits the negro race by reason of the

fact that they will be afforded schools and churches which are accessible, whereas the scattering of the population makes it impossible for them to get full benefit of the separate schools."[3]

Living conditions in the black villages were intolerable when spring rains flooded houses and washed away garden spots. More than once young Jimmy Stewart and his family had to be rescued from rushing floodwaters by firemen in boats.

Living along the North Canadian had its benefits however. Jimmy learned to swim at Sandy Bend on the river, just north of the present Exchange Avenue Bridge, and at a place on the river known as Gargoly, the only public swimming area for blacks in early Oklahoma City.

Ralph Ellison, winner of the 1952
National Book Award for his first novel,
Invisible Man. Ellison and Jimmy grew
up in the Sand Town area of Oklahoma
City. (Courtesy *The Daily Oklahoman.*)

The old Western League baseball park was near Sandy Bend. Jimmy and his friends watched baseball games from a nearby hill. The price of admission to a game was only a nickel, but a nickel was scarce and was better used for a loaf of bread. Jimmy loved the carnivals that frequented the old show grounds between Reno Street and Exchange Avenue.

Most of Jimmy's early life revolved around the Orchard Park Elementary School. In fact, the school was the center of most social, civic and educational activities of the black families in West Town. Jimmy developed a competitive spirit by playing baseball for the Orchard Park team which regularly competed against teams from Douglass, Dunbar, and Sand Town.

Down the street from the Stewart house in West Town lived the Ellison family who had a skinny son named Ralph, two years younger than Jimmy. Ralph was an aspiring trumpeter whose practice sessions could be heard for blocks. Jimmy was in the third grade the first time he met young Ellison at the corner of Main and Brauer streets. Ellison had recently lost his father and lived with an aunt.

After suppers of "black-eyed peas and turnip greens, cracklin' bread and buttermilk, lemonade and sweet potato cobbler," young

Ellison, oversupplied with bursting energy, locked his lips to his trumpet and tried to mimic Louie Armstrong.[4]

Jimmy and Ellison played music together in the Douglass School band. One of the teachers with a military background who helped drill the band was Johnson Chesnut Whittaker. Professor Whittaker had a storied past. He was one of the first blacks admitted to West Point but was court-martialed in his senior year as a result of a trumped-up, false charge that he faked an assault on himself to make the military academy look bad. More than a century later, in 1995, President Bill Clinton presented Whittaker's descendants with his second lieutenant bars and granted Whittaker a commission from West Point.[5]

Whittaker worked his band members hard, and it paid off. Jimmy, Ellison, and other members of the Douglass band stole the show in 1926 when they marched in the Oklahoma City Boys Day Parade, the first time black boys were allowed to participate in the annual event.

Ellison, who laid his trumpet aside for a typewriter, became one of America's finest writers. In 1952, his first book, *Invisible Man,* received almost unprecedented critical acclaim, winning the National Book Award in 1953 and the National Newspaper Publishers Award in 1954. It was honored by a Book Week poll in 1965 as "the most distinguished single work published in the last twenty years."[6]

Invisible Man is a powerful book that more than one critic has called the most profound exploration of the black experience in America. It is the story of a southern black man who searches for meaning and identity in life, moving to the North, where he is still invisible in the eyes of whites even though he is self-reliant and ingenious. The book contains many of Ellison's recollections from his childhood in West Town. Ellison died April 16, 1994.

Education for black children in Oklahoma City in 1918 was inferior to training provided at schools for white children. The first school for blacks was opened in March, 1891 in a two-room house at California Street and Harvey Avenue. Jefferson Davis Randolph, a graduate of Roger Williams College in Tennessee and grandfather of Dr. W. H. Slaughter, was the first teacher of the school. As attendance grew, school officials enclosed an open shed attached to the house and added another room, and another teacher, Drucilla Dunjee.

Randolph and Dunjee taught the usual subjects, reading, writing, and arithmetic and more. There was plenty of land around the school house so Randolph taught the boys to plow the ground and plant vegetable gardens. When the crops were harvested, Dunjee instructed the girls on the art of canning. Sewing and printing classes also were offered.

Before the turn of the century, a two-story frame school was built in the 400 block of California Street. It was named for Frederick Douglass, noted abolitionist, orator, and statesman. When the school burned in 1903, students at Douglass were moved to the basement of a school at Reno and Walnut. A new school was eventually built on a large plot of land between Reno and California, Walnut and Central.

Harriet Price Johnson-Jacobson left Douglass to become the first principal at Orchard Park after 1910. Other early black schools in Oklahoma City were Choctaw, in the 100 block of West Choctaw Street in South Town; Dunbar, in the 1500 block of Northeast Fourth Street; Carver, in Sand Town; Bryant (later Inman Page), at Second and Geary streets; Benjamin Bannaker, in Walnut Grove; Carter G. Woodson, between Harvey and Hudson on Southwest Thirteenth Street; and Beth (later Truman), at Twelfth and Kelham streets.[7]

After completing the sixth grade at Orchard Park, Jimmy enrolled at distant Douglass Junior High School. There were closer junior high schools, but those schools were reserved for white students.

Segregation was cruel. It gave Jimmy an early social consciousness. If he and his mother rode on the street car, they were forced to sit in the rear. By 1921 there were more than 12,000 blacks in Oklahoma City. Most could not afford a car or truck and had to rely on the street car system. Anton H. Classen and John Shartel operated the Oklahoma Railway Company, which ran street cars

Jimmy graduated from high school in May, 1931 in Wichita, Kansas and was ready to take on the world.

from Guthrie to Norman (the Interurban) and from El Reno to northeast Oklahoma City.

The street car system became such an important part of Jimmy's life that he used "stop" numbers on the street car line to describe parts of Oklahoma City for the remainder of his life. He never referred to the "northeast" or "northwest" sides of town. He might instead talk about going fishing at "stop 29."

Each street car was equipped with an adjustable bar that divided white and black passengers. Oklahoma City's black newspaper, *The Black Dispatch*, often printed complaints from blacks who had to stand in the aisles, packed like sardines, even though seats were vacant in the section reserved for whites. The newspaper said, "When a Negro sits on a vacant seat in the white section, the trouble starts." [8]

Segregation in transportation, an issue that Jimmy would valiantly fight against later in life, was an embarrassing reality from the time of statehood. The first bill introduced in the state legislature after Oklahoma became a state in November, 1907, was a Jim Crow law requiring railroads to provide separate cars for blacks

and whites. The term "Jim Crow" came from a comedy act from the 1830s when a white comedian painted his face black and called his character "Jim Crow." The term came to symbolize black or segregated, such as a Jim Crow park, school, train, or hotel.

In 1928 Maggie Stewart and Jimmy moved north to Wichita, Kansas, to live with her oldest daughter, Ella Gravelly. All of Maggie's children except Jimmy had left home. Jimmy, at age 16, enrolled in the tenth grade at Wichita High School East, the city's only high school. The next year he transferred to a new school, Wichita High School North.

Jimmy was always above average in athletics but had not tried out for team sports at Douglass High School in Oklahoma City.

In Wichita, in the fall of 1929, Jimmy made the final cut for the varsity football squad out of 104 recruits. When his name was called, a big, red-headed Kansas boy, "Red" Winters, asked a friend, "Did that nigger make the team?" Jimmy turned his head and ignored the remark. He vowed to work hard and prove that his color was irrelevant to his value to the team.

A few weeks later during a tough game against Arkansas City, Kansas, Jimmy looked at the stands and saw not one black person in attendance. He noticed a confrontation between Winters and a member of the opposing team. Jimmy overheard his newly-made white friend say, "And you better not bother him!" Jimmy had won the respect of the white players on the Wichita High School North squad. On the field, Jimmy was the only member of his team's starting backfield to make the All-City team.

Jimmy (bottom left) was the only black member of the 1930 Wichita High School North football squad. Jimmy was named to the All-City backfield.

The first sign that Jimmy would spend his life fighting discrimination came during his senior year in high school. He never forgot the day he sat in the high school auditorium and heard a visiting chorus of all-white singers bellow the words from "Ol' Man River," from the musical "Showboat": "Niggers all work on the Mississippi. . . Niggers all work while the white folks play. . . " Jimmy, 17-years-old and proud of the black color of his skin, marched to the principal's office and diplomatically protested the humiliation he suffered from the use of the song. The principal listened and promised the words would be changed in future performances.

With his first attempt at combating discrimination a success, Jimmy moved on to another project, to convince school officials to allow black students to swim in the Wichita High School North pool. Part of the credit given for gym classes was for swimming, but black students could not use the high school pool. After Jimmy had a frank talk with the principal, black students were allowed to swim in the pool on Fridays. However, the principal ordered the pool drained on Saturdays so white students could again swim Monday through Thursday.

From left to right: Jimmy Stewart, Mae Lois, Stewart's sister Essie, and her husband Bervis McBride, Sr.

Don Stewart, left, with first-cousins Bervis, Jr. and Bobbie Jean McBride, 1938.

Jimmy was not a star player in high school, but certainly was above average in football, basketball, and track. He probably deserved a scholarship to the University of Kansas, but when he graduated from high school in May, 1931, Kansas, as well as many states, did not allow blacks to enroll in its state universities.

Jimmy's fate turned back to Oklahoma, to Langston University, where black students were welcome. Langston University was established as Oklahoma's Colored Agricultural and Normal University in the pioneer community of Langston, east of Guthrie in Logan County. A land-grant college authorized by the Morrill Acts of 1862 and 1890, Langston was one of 17 colleges established across the South in states like Oklahoma who dared not admit blacks to its main universities.

Jimmy was awarded a partial football scholarship at Langston for his freshman year. He entered school in September, 1931 and played under new coach Caesar Felton "Zip" Gayles who guided Langston's pigskin program for almost 30 years.

It was at Langston that Jimmy first realized how blatantly unfair "separate but equal" education was for black students. Oklahoma's constitution mandated separate facilities for blacks at all levels of education, from elementary schools to universities. The state simply followed the national rule of law that separate but equal educational facilities fulfilled the federal constitutional guarantee of equal protection under the law as defined by the United States Supreme Court in the case of *Plessy v. Ferguson* in 1896.

Oklahoma, as other southern states, claimed to offer separate but equal educational opportunities to all races. In reality the doctrine of "separate but equal" was a lot more separate than it ever was equal.[9]

The 1930 appropriation for Langston University from the state legislature was $94,000, or $80 per student. The per capita appropriation for students at Oklahoma A&M at Stillwater, an all-white school, was $160.30. Jimmy observed the poor and aging facilities and equipment that the faculty at Langston had to work with. His high school in Wichita had better laboratory equipment than did Langston. The pitiful, neglected state of Langston University had prompted the editor of *The Black Dispatch* to surmise that if the legislature visited Langston, they would either improve it or abolish it.[11]

Conditions at Langston made it easier for Jimmy to get involved in the advocacy of civil rights. After one year at Langston, with his attitude that he "knew more than the teachers,"[12] Jimmy quit college and drifted back to Oklahoma City to establish a life of helping others seek equality.

Jimmy soon fell in love with a beautiful 17-year-old girl, Mae Belle Hayes, of mixed Choctaw-Chickasaw Indian and black parentage. Mae Belle lived on Northeast Eighth Street with her aunt because her parents were deceased. After a whirlwind romance, Jimmy and Mae Belle, still in high school, ran away and were married in late 1932. On November 14, 1933, a bouncing baby boy, Don Gilbert Stewart, was born.

Jimmy and Mae Belle's marriage lasted only a few months after the baby was born. They were divorced in 1934. Mae Belle stayed in Oklahoma City for a few years before moving to Missouri.

Jimmy always played a major role in Don's life. Don completed a successful tour in the Navy and worked for the United States Postal Service and the United States Department of Labor after graduating from Rockhurst College, a Jesuit school in Kansas City, Missouri. He inherited his father's love for jazz. For years he featured selections from his vast collection of jazz recordings on a daily radio show in Kansas City.

TWO
DEEP DEUCE

YOU COULD BUY a large glass of tea for a nickel. A quarter would get you a plate lunch piled high with chitlins and peach cobbler at the Midway Cafe. The strains of jazz and the blues somehow escaped the smoke-filled clubs out onto the sidewalks along the 300 block of Northeast Second Street in Oklahoma City. The setting was "Deep Second" or "Deep Deuce," certainly the center of black culture in Oklahoma City in the 1930s.

Deep Deuce attracted Jimmy Stewart to its hotels, theaters, dance halls, pool halls, and jazz clubs. Nights were alive on Second Street. The streets and sidewalks in the commercial area were crowded with people.

Television had yet to be born and radio was in its infancy. Slaughter Hall became the most popular dance hall for blacks. Jimmy moved into a house on Douglass Street and landed a job as manager of the Jewel Theater. The position only paid a few dollars a week, just enough to live in a decent apartment, eat good at the world-class cafes like Ruby's Grill or the Midway Cafe, and take in some of America's greatest music.

Music made its home on Deep Deuce. On any given night outstanding musicians who went on to national and world fame in jazz circles played along Second Street. Charlie Christian, Jimmy Rushing, and Claude "Fiddler" Williams started on Deep Deuce. If a national jazz band needed a musician, its leader headed for Second Street. Even Count Basie recruited band members from Deuce.[1]

Charlie Christian, a Texas native, grew up in Oklahoma City and learned to make music on the guitar from his father, a blind street singer. Christian, who eventually died of tuberculosis blamed on years spent in a wooden Oklahoma City slum apartment house, is credited with influencing most of the great jazz guitarists of the mid-twentieth century. Christian attended Douglass School with Jimmy and Ralph Ellison, who both knew Christian would turn out to be a great guitarist because he spent most of his time in the manual-training classes building guitars out of cigar boxes. Ellison wrote, "With Christian the guitar found its jazz voice. With his entry into the jazz circles his musical intelligence was able to exert its influence upon his peers and to affect the course of the future development of jazz."[2]

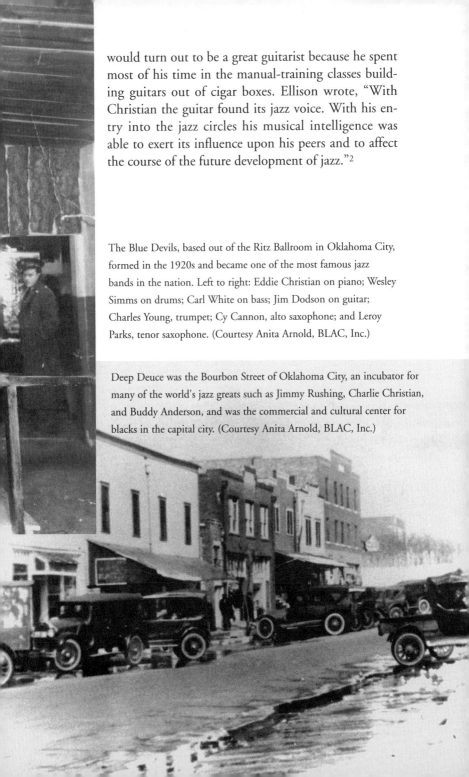

The Blue Devils, based out of the Ritz Ballroom in Oklahoma City, formed in the 1920s and became one of the most famous jazz bands in the nation. Left to right: Eddie Christian on piano; Wesley Simms on drums; Carl White on bass; Jim Dodson on guitar; Charles Young, trumpet; Cy Cannon, alto saxophone; and Leroy Parks, tenor saxophone. (Courtesy Anita Arnold, BLAC, Inc.)

Deep Deuce was the Bourbon Street of Oklahoma City, an incubator for many of the world's jazz greats such as Jimmy Rushing, Charlie Christian, and Buddy Anderson, and was the commercial and cultural center for blacks in the capital city. (Courtesy Anita Arnold, BLAC, Inc.)

The Ideal Orchestra and the famous Blue Devils played at the Aldridge Theater, Ruby's Grill, or Slaughter Hall almost every night of the week. When Jimmy was not working at the Jewel Theater, he was part of the Deep Deuce culture. His favorite nightspot was James Simpson's Club.

Jimmy particularly enjoyed Jimmy Rushing's family. Rushing's father, bandsman Andrew Rushing, played the tuba. Jimmy Rushing learned to play the piano and violin by ear and studied music at Douglass High School. He sang and cooked and poured root beer at his father's lunchroom on Second Street. He was short and heavy and became known as "Mr. Five-by-Five." Rushing became internationally famous as a vocalist for the Count Basie Band from 1935 to 1950.[3]

Ralph Ellison memorialized Rushing's voice in an article in the *Saturday Review* in 1958:

> In the old days the voice was high and clear and poignantly lyrical. Steel-bright in its upper range and, at its best, silky smooth, it was possessed of a purity somehow impervious to both the stress of singing above a twelve-piece band and the urgency of Rushing's own blazing fervor. On dance nights, when you stood on the rise of the school grounds two blocks to the east, you could hear it jetting from the dance hall like a blue flame in the dark; now soaring high above the trumpets and trombones, now skimming the froth of reeds and rhythm as it called some woman's anguished name—or demanded in a high, thin, passionately lyrical line, "Baaaaay-bay, Bay-aaaay-bay! Tell me what's the matter now!"—above the shouting of the swinging band.

Music historian William W. Savage, Jr. called Oklahoma the "matrix whence came much of the best of American jazz."[5]

Jimmy's nightly trek to Second Street was medicine for the glum news he heard each day about the Great Depression. The economic woes had begun with the stock market crash in 1929 and worsened in the early 1930s as banks closed, millions lost

Charlie Christian, left, revolutionized the electric guitar as a solo instrument and influenced many jazz and popular music guitarists. In 1939, Benny Goodman, right, leader of one of the most famous big bands of the swing era, crossed color lines and introduced Christian to America. Since 1985, the Charlie Christian Jazz Festival is an annual celebration in Oklahoma City. (Courtesy Anita Arnold, BLAC, Inc.)

their jobs, and farm foreclosures in Oklahoma reached an all-time high. Jimmy later recalled that the four-four beat on Second Street drove the feelings of hopelessness away, even if just for the night.

If Jimmy still had a few cents at the end of a night's music festivities, he trudged to Well's Chili Parlor, where musical giants who had finished their gig enjoyed big bowls of chili laced with onions and hot sauce.

On Second Street Jimmy met many of the characters and leaders who helped shape his life. Roscoe Dunjee founded the black newspaper, *The Black Dispatch*, on Second Street in 1914. Dunjee, with the force of his editorial page, became the major voice for blacks in their fight for equality in Oklahoma. He was afraid of no one. His ink was piercing, yet compassionate. His language was precise and his positions courageous. Dunjee was relentless in his fight against discrimination, hate, and prejudice. When Dunjee died in 1965, Jimmy wrote a tribute to the late editor in *The Black Dispatch*, "He had no peer on the subject closest to him, the awakening of America to the injustice suffered by Negroes, and seeking solutions to grant them full citizenship and all its privileges."[6]

Roscoe Dunjee, editor of *The Black Dispatch,* was one of the nation's strongest voices for equal rights from 1915 to the middle of the century. Jimmy was proud to be called "a disciple of Dunjee." (Courtesy *The Daily Oklahoman.*)

Two black physicians had a positive impact on young Jimmy's life. Pioneer black physician W. H. Slaughter worked tirelessly on civic projects to better the life of his patients and neighbors. As an entrepreneur, Dr. Slaughter built and operated Slaughter Hall, one of the more popular entertainment spots for blacks in Oklahoma City. Dr. Slaughter, orphaned at age five and raised by an ex-slave aunt, graduated from medical school in Tennessee and came to Oklahoma in 1903. He was the first president of the Oklahoma Medical, Dental, and Pharmaceutical Association, the black state medical society.

When Dr. Slaughter died in 1952, *The Black Dispatch* editor Dunjee called him "easily the outstanding citizen of his city and state" and lauded him for offering advice and counsel to young families in trouble. "While he had an uncanny capacity and ability to drive a good business deal, his patients knew that he would serve them without money and without price, and many a home of an early day settler in the Sooner capital was saved for them through the big heart and neighborly assistance of Dr. Slaughter."[7]

Dr. W. L. Haywood was one of Jimmy's tutors in working for civil rights and equality for blacks in Oklahoma. Dr. Haywood, who came to Oklahoma City in 1908 from Tennessee, built Utopia Hospital, the first black hospital in Oklahoma City.

Jimmy loved to frequent Hallie Richardson's book and magazine store on Second Street. Richardson, fondly called "Fat Hallie" by his friends and enemies alike, more than once loaned Jimmy a few dollars until pay day.

A pharmacist, Dr. W. L. Vaughn, also had a positive influence on young Jimmy. Vaughn moved to Oklahoma City from Tennessee and operated a successful pharmacy. He was active in the Negro Business League. Jimmy also enjoyed a mutual friendship with Dewey Moore, a pharmacist on Fourth Street.

James Brooks, known as "Doebelly," was Jimmy's friend. Brooks had lived on Second Street since 1923 and made his living shining shoes. Incidentally, he got his nickname from eating raw cookie dough. Doebelly was a purveyor of shines, shoes, news, and snapshots. *The Black Dispatch* columnist "Wild Bill" Bebop later wrote of Doebelly, "His appearance has always evoked an attitude of mirthful enjoyment. He is known in the entertainment circle on a national scale. With his camera this natural comic has made the scene and made it merry. He can smile you out of your right arm."[8] Doebelly later occupied the old building at 300 Northeast Second Street that had been the early home of *The Black Dispatch*.

Stewart always loved hats. If he dressed up for church or for parties, he was seldom seen without his best hat.

Walter J. Edwards moved to Oklahoma City in 1915 and started a baggage company. He built one of the city's first drive-in filling stations after the advent of the automobile. It was the junk business, however, that made Edwards a rich man. Edwards also built the Edwards Addition and the Edwards Hospital. Jimmy watched men like Edwards use much of their wealth to help their fellow citizens who were less fortunate. It was a lesson Jimmy kept close to heart his entire life.

Jimmy followed in the footsteps of two ministers who gave much of their time to civil rights issues. Reverend E. W. Perry came to Oklahoma City in 1915 with his wife and six children to became pastor of the Tabernacle Baptist Church. He was president of the Oklahoma Baptist Convention for more than 40 years.

Reverend J. W. Johnson, president of the Ministerial Alliance, worked with Jimmy on early projects to improve the economy and living conditions of the eastside. Johnson pastored St. John Baptist Church.

Jimmy thought the most important woman in Oklahoma City was probably Zelia N. Page Breaux, the music supervisor for the Colored Oklahoma City Public Schools. Mrs. Breaux, the daughter of Langston University's first president, Dr. Inman Page, became head of the music department at Langston at the age of 18. Twenty years later, she accepted the music job in Oklahoma City. At Douglass High School, she taught many of the great jazz musicians that grew up in Oklahoma City. Her band was one of the best among black schools anywhere in America, and was invited to the World's Fair in Chicago in 1933 where it appeared on a national radio broadcast.

Jimmy respected Mrs. Breaux's absolute devotion for teaching her students to be proud of their heritage and proud enough to do their very best in each task of life.

The slim pay at the Jewel Theater forced Jimmy to look elsewhere for work. He waited tables at the Oklahoma City Golf and Country Club in Nichols Hills and became head waiter at Twin Hills Golf and Country Club.

In the summer of 1936 Jimmy tripled his normal wages by

serving food at Billy Rose's Casa Manna Restaurant in Fort Worth, Texas, during the Texas Centennial Celebration.

When Jimmy returned to Oklahoma City, he became captain of banquet service for the Oklahoma Biltmore Hotel on Grand Avenue in downtown Oklahoma City. The 33-story hotel, completed in 1930, was the toast of the town. Its board of directors included Charles Colcord, W. T. Hales, W. R. Ramsey, R. J. Edwards, and other community leaders.

As a part-time butler, Jimmy served many of the wealthy families of Oklahoma City. He waited on guests at family gatherings and parties. It was a strategic role for Jimmy, who would later influence the leaders of the community, some of whom he had waited tables for at their parties decades before.

At the Biltmore, Jimmy became friends with a customer named Thomas H. Sterling, an official of Oklahoma Natural Gas Company. In 1937 Sterling made an offer to Jimmy that would change the course of Oklahoma history.

THREE
OKLAHOMA
NATURAL GAS

OKLAHOMA CITY had a population of only 32,000 in 1906 when two farsighted Oklahoma City lawyers formed a company to deliver natural gas to residents of the capital city. Dennis T. Flynn and C.B. Ames called their company Oklahoma Natural Gas (ONG) and were granted a 20-year charter to serve Oklahoma City. In 1926 America's oil and gas industry claimed Tulsa as its capital and ONG moved its home office from Oklahoma City to Tulsa.[1] ONG became a division of ONEOK, Inc. in the 1980s.

Jimmy's first contact with ONG resulted from his brief stint as owner and operator of the College Inn, a small hamburger stand he built on the vacant lot next to the Jewel Theater. Roy B. Deal, Sr., an ONG employee, showed up one morning for an inspection and cited Jimmy for using a non-registered gas meter to supply fuel for his hamburger grill. After Deal left, Oscar Lamb, who operated a bakery across the street, ranted and raved about big utilities not hiring black people.

The next day Jimmy arrived at the central ONG office to leave a deposit for gas service for his hamburger venture and to lodge a complaint about the lack of blacks working for ONG. He met with district manager Thomas Sterling.

Sterling was impressed with Jimmy's calmness and mannerly approach to a sensitive problem. He promised Jimmy that if he would work to convince voters to support ONG in an upcoming franchise election in Oklahoma City, blacks would be considered for employment.

Jimmy returned to the eastside ready to campaign for the ONG franchise approval. His optimism was shattered when he tried to convert a leading Methodist minister on the issue. The minister pointed to an electric lineman on a nearby pole, "Son, you see those men down there. Negroes will never have those kind of jobs and I haven't got time for your foolishness." [2]

Despite the initial setback, Jimmy believed Sterling's promise and supported ONG in its successful bid to win approval of the voters of Oklahoma City for continued exclusive natural gas service.

After Jimmy began his job at the Biltmore Hotel, he often served Sterling at Rotary Club luncheons. Sterling noticed Jimmy's manners, his friendliness, and his obvious good work ethic. One day, out of the blue, Sterling offered Jimmy a job as a janitor at ONG. Jimmy was looking for steady work, but the pay at ONG was far less than the above-average wages he was earning at the Biltmore. In fact, Jimmy figured that he earned more in one day at the Biltmore than he would bring home in one week at ONG. After a couple of sleepless nights considering other factors, such as stability and growth potential, Jimmy accepted Sterling's offer. He reported for duty at ONG June 1, 1937.

Roy B. Deal, Sr. was Jimmy's first supervisor at ONG. Deal, the chief clerk of the Oklahoma City office, was understanding and helpful to Jimmy, who admitted he was "not much of a janitor."

Roy B. Deal, Sr. was the longtime personnel director at Oklahoma Natural Gas Company. He often sought Stewart's advice on how to handle sensitive employee problems. (Courtesy *The Daily Oklahoman.*)

Jimmy's love for a good discussion on almost any topic worked to his advantage at ONG. Oklahoma City ONG Vice President George Frederickson and Jimmy spent many hours talking about everything from "peanuts to the pope."[3] Frederickson encouraged Jimmy to stand up for what he believed and to get involved in political campaigns and civic activities. For many years Jimmy sought Frederickson's counsel when making important decisions in public battles. "Uncle George" Frederickson was a popular ONG leader whose activities bolstered the gas company's image in Oklahoma City. The fieldhouse at Oklahoma City University is named for Frederickson.

By 1939 Jimmy was well-known in political and civic club circles in Oklahoma City. ONG paid for Jimmy to join many of the civic clubs on the eastside. *The Black Dispatch* editor Roscoe Dunjee asked Jimmy to write a weekly column for the newspaper. The column was called "Jimmy Says." It was a menagerie of the happenings on the eastside. Some examples of Jimmy's writings and ramblings from his first few columns in 1939:

Saw Reggy Pittman and Orbery Else in a pushing match in front of "Fats" Spence's place the other day. This could have well been billed as the heavyweight pushing match of Deep Second Street, as Hallie Richardson was the referee.

The sun must have gone down on Bonner's muffins the other evening at Lyons cafe. They kept the butter that I attempted to spread on them chilled as well as any modern ice box could have.

Saw Cecil Parker at Bailey's Inn while on my jaunt. Cecil is from the hills of Okfuskee County and really knows how to imitate a wild Indian when he gets nine feet instead of four feet five.

What's the matter with Douglass? She's all right. Who said so? The people who help fill the stands and show the boys that they are really behind them.

Have you heard Charles Christian on the Camel Caravan yet? Charles is one of our local boys that Benny Goodman is featuring with his newly formed sextet.

My boss, Mr. Thomas Sterling, asked his new secretary to try to be a little more personal in her correspondence, especially between his office and the home office in Tulsa. Next day in a letter to Mr. Joseph Bowes, our president, she closed by saying: "We are all getting along fine over here. How is your wife and kiddies? Say Mr. Bowes, I wonder if you could let me have a five-spot until pay day?"

I wonder what happy company is paying Ballard, the barber over at the Golden Oak, to wear that derby. Some people say individuality, but I'll stick to convention.

If war in Europe is going to affect our sugar prices so quickly, I'll advise the fellows to get on better terms with these "sweet things."[4]

Jimmy always ended his weekly column with, "You make it, I write it, let's have it."

Jimmy became more popular than ever and received invitations to almost every social, church, and civic event whose participants wanted Jimmy to mention them in his column.

Jimmy and Dunjee became close friends almost immediately after Jimmy began writing the weekly column in 1939. Jimmy spent countless hours at the newspaper office listening to Dunjee relate the stories of early anti-discrimination battles in Oklahoma

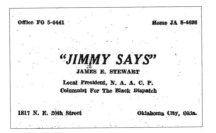

Stewart's card announced his position with the NAACP and promoted his column in *The Black Dispatch*.

Above: Stewart, left, with his staff at the ONG branch office. Left: One of Stewart's responsibilities as manager of the ONG office in northeast Oklahoma City was to promote gas appliances.

City. Jimmy worshipped Dunjee, calling him "the most unselfish patriot the great southwestern part of our nation ever produced in the field of human relations and civil rights," and "the most thought provoking editorial writer of his day."[5] Jimmy referred to Dunjee as his "father-confessor."

Jimmy was only 27 when Dunjee took him under his wing. The editor began inviting Jimmy to accompany him to rallies of black citizens who were upset and frustrated with Jim Crow policies of city and state governments.

One of the first civil rights battles Jimmy became involved in was a protest against Oklahoma City Municipal Zoo officials who prohibited black parents and their children from visiting the zoo. Jimmy and Dunjee attended a Park Board meeting and won concessions from city leaders who set aside Thursday of each week as "Negro Day" at the zoo.

Dunjee poked fun at city officials in a July 29, 1939, editorial, "One would assume that the natural aversion implied, which white folk have for getting in close proximity to Negroes, would cause every Nordic to shun looking in the direction of wild animals on Thursday. Surely, with its advertisement in the papers, together with a solemn city ordinance prohibiting intermingling of the races, one would assume nothing but a dark cloud would hover over Lincoln Park and lake on Thursday."[6]

Jimmy shared most of Dunjee's positions on equal education, voting rights, fair criminal trials, and equal job opportunities for blacks in Oklahoma City. Dunjee sponsored Jimmy as a member of the National Negro Business League chapter on the eastside.

Jimmy's friends and supervisors at ONG supported his involvement in the zoo controversy and other causes of the day. They knew he was slow to anger and would not start a fight that he could not justify, and win.

In the summer of 1940, Jimmy's supervisor, Roy B. Deal, Sr., recommended to ONG home office officials in Tulsa that an ONG branch office be opened on the eastside of Oklahoma City. Deal presented his idea to Oakah L. Jones, the company's secretary-treasurer. Jones, who later served as president of a large Canadian gas utility, was aware of Jimmy's civic work and approved Deal's idea for a new office.

In September, 1940, Jimmy was appointed manager of the ONG eastside office, despite warnings from some white leaders that the move would hurt ONG. Jimmy was one of the first blacks to serve in a management position for a public utility in the southwestern United States.

FOUR
THE NAACP

ONE OF THE FIRST ORGANIZATIONS Stewart joined upon his return to Oklahoma City was the local chapter of the National Association for the Advancement of Colored People (NAACP).

Sixty people, black and white, had organized the NAACP at a meeting in New York City on President Abraham Lincoln's birthday in 1909. From its inception, the organization's purpose was to alleviate the untenable conditions under which most black Americans lived.

Oklahoma blacks began the fight in the courts for their civil rights shortly after Oklahoma statehood. The Constitutional League, led by Dr. William H. Jernigan, made one of the nation's initial attempts to strike down Jim Crow laws in 1908.

One of the first actual victories for black Americans in anti-discrimination court battles was in an Oklahoma case in 1915. In *Guinn v. United States,* the United States Supreme Court invalidated Oklahoma's grandfather clause which basically prevented blacks from voting in local and state elections.

Oklahoma's constitution, adopted in 1907, prohibited the passage of laws that would prevent any citizen's right to vote based on color or race. However, when black Republican Albert Comstock Hamlin was elected to the state House of Representatives in 1908 from Logan County, white leaders introduced State Question 17, an obvious and blatant attempt to disenfranchise Oklahoma blacks.

Oklahoma voters approved the state question in 1910 and amended the state constitution to mandate a literacy test for voters. The amendment required a voter to be able to read a section of the state constitution, but exempt any person whose ancestors could legally vote before 1866, the year blacks were granted the right to vote. The so-called grandfather clause grandfathered in all white voters and discriminated against the many black voters who could not read.

After the grandfather clause was voided by the United States Supreme Court, Oklahoma leaders continued to try to exclude blacks from the election process. The state legislature passed a law that required eligible voters to be registered within a 12-day period or be declared ineligible.

The NAACP challenged the Oklahoma action. In 1939, in *Lane v. Wilson,* the United States Supreme Court held that the Oklahoma law violated the Fifteenth Amendment. Justice Felix Frankfurter wrote, "The Amendment nullifies sophisticated as well as simple-minded modes of discrimination."

Dr. William H. Jernigan, pastor of the Tabernacle Baptist Church, contacted the NAACP headquarters in New York City in 1912 in order to inquire about setting up a local chapter of the organization. The Oklahoma City Branch of the NAACP which resulted was one of the first local chapters of the national movement. It was organized in June, 1913.

In that same year, Dr. Jernigan joined forces with H. A. Berry, a teacher at Douglass High School who also was an agent for the NAACP's official publication, *The Crisis.* Together with Reverend J. N. Abby, pastor of the Avery Chapel American Methodist Episcopal Church, and J. H. A. Brazelton, principal of Douglass High School, Jernigan and Berry formed a group that met at the home of Mrs. Harriet Price Jacobson on Second Street. They elected Dr. A. Baxter Whitby, of the Tabernacle Baptist Church, first president of the Oklahoma City branch of the NAACP. Mrs. Jacobson was elected secretary, a position she held for more than 30 years.

In its first few years, the local NAACP chapter was only moderately successful in black causes. In 1915, after *The Black Dis-*

patch editor Roscoe Dunjee and attorney W. H. Twine took up the case of a 14-year-old boy who had been sentenced to death for the murder of a white woman, the NAACP became a force to reckon with in the Sooner State. In the name of the NAACP, Dunjee and Twine raised contributions from all over the state to fight the death sentence given to young Elias Ridge. Their efforts paid off. The Criminal Appeals Court commuted the youngster's punishment to life in prison.

In 1919 the NAACP local group was successful in defending shoe cobbler William Floyd, who was arrested seven times in one day for violating the city's housing segregation ordinance.

Throughout the 1920s the NAACP was active in civil rights causes. Dr. S. C. Snelson and Reverend W. F. Houston served as president of the local branch. Adequate housing was a major issue because blacks had outgrown their traditional communities and sought homes in areas occupied by whites. The bulk of the black population lived in an area south of Grand Avenue and north of the North Canadian River. Other scattered groups of blacks lived in the Fairgrounds, West Town, Wheeler Park, Sand Town, and Brickyard (Northwest Tenth Street) additions.

After World War I there was a tightening of available housing for blacks. Stewart wrote about the trend years later in *The Black Dispatch* in a story which recited the history of the local branch of the NAACP, "Unfortunately some Negroes were a part and parcel of the unholy alliance of city planners and realtors to keep the Negro in his place. They had to be dealt with like the rest and the branch had on many occasions to go up town and help undo some things which our people had agreed to which were against the best interests of the community as a whole."[1]

The NAACP became the official watchdog for the welfare of blacks in Oklahoma. While civil rights was its primary function, the Oklahoma City branch often found itself as the "Mother Hubbard" of Negro activities and endeavor in the community.[2] The organization urged parents to make certain their children attended school, sought support of the Community Chest, and petitioned the city to hire blacks in city health department positions.

In April, 1929, local NAACP branches in Oklahoma City, Guthrie, Chickasha, Tulsa, and Muskogee formed a statewide organization known as the Oklahoma Conference of Branches. It was the nation's first state conference of NAACP local branches. Other states soon followed Oklahoma's lead and patterned their organizations after the Oklahoma Conference. Roscoe Dunjee was elected state president, a position he held for 20 years.

In 1931 the NAACP rallied behind Jess Hollins, a Creek County black who was sentenced to die in the electric chair for the rape of a white woman. Hollins was drunk and confessed to the crime. District Judge Gaylord Wilcox said he saw no need for a confessed guilty person to need a lawyer and pronounced the death penalty for Hollins.

A new trial was granted and the case was moved to Okmulgee County. Even though 17 percent of the citizens of Okmulgee County were black, blacks were excluded from the jury. Hollins was found guilty by the all-white jury and again faced the death sentence. After years of legal wrangling, the United States Supreme Court used the Hollins case to forever bar states from excluding blacks from juries. Oklahoma black leaders had won a major legal battle in the fight for equality.

In the 1930s Stewart became an active member of the local branch and served on several committees. He headed up the 1938 Community Chest drive on the eastside. He was elected vice president in 1942, nominated for the position by editor Dunjee. Stewart was absent from the meeting and found out about his election the next morning over coffee with Dunjee.

A month later, the president of the local branch, a young attorney, left town. Stewart and the executive committee met to decide who should be the new president. Dunjee intervened and told Stewart, "You're the president. Take over your duties now!" Stewart accepted Dunjee's counsel and on February 8, 1942, took over the reins of what would become one of the most active branches of the NAACP in the nation.

Through Dunjee, Stewart developed a close friendship with a young New York City special counsel of the NAACP, Thurgood

Marshall, who had been born in Maryland in 1908. As a civil rights lawyer, he won 29 of 32 cases he argued before the United States Supreme Court, including the *Brown v. Board of Education* decision of 1954 which banned racial segregation in public schools. Marshall was appointed by President Lyndon B. Johnson as the first black member of the United States Supreme Court in 1967.

In later years, Stewart and Mae Lois, his second wife, visited the Marshalls when touring the nation's capital. In the early years of their friendship, when Marshall came to Oklahoma City, it was usually Mae Lois who served as his chauffeur. Marshall always brought a legal secretary with him and traditionally stayed with the Stewarts and other black families on the eastside, lodging made necessary by the refusal of downtown Oklahoma City hotels to serve blacks.

Marshall loved Western movies. At the end of a hard day's legal maneuvering, he often asked Stewart to "let him off at the movies." Marshall also liked the taste of Oklahoma moonshine whiskey. Often, when bootleggers knew Marshall was coming to town, they delivered a case or two of "shine" for consumption by Marshall and his company of lawyers, secretaries, and admirers.

Stewart's first legal case with attorney Marshall involved a criminal defendant from Choctaw County, Oklahoma. Dunjee and Stewart raised money to bring Marshall to Oklahoma to defend W. D. Lyons who was accused of murdering a white man, his wife, and two children near Hugo and burning their house to hide the crime.

Dunjee and Stewart drove Marshall to Hugo, in Oklahoma's Little Dixie, for the trial. When they arrived in town, more than 1,500 whites and blacks surrounded the county courthouse, waiting for a chance to crowd into the tiny courtroom.

Racial tensions ran high in Hugo. There was an unsubstantiated, well-published rumor that blacks had smuggled weapons into town from Oklahoma City and Tulsa.

Marshall's safety was paramount to Dunjee, Stewart, and local black leaders in Hugo. Elaborate precautions, such as having Marshall sleep at a different well-guarded home every night, were taken.

Marshall had the local crowd and jury spell-bound with his cross-examination of the state's witnesses. He forced local law officers to admit they had stacked the bloody and charred bones of the victims on the defendant's body to procure the original confession. Marshall argued that a second, voluntary confession was made by Lyons because of his fear of "sadism" and "police brutality."[3] Members of the jury failed to heed Marshall's pleas. They convicted Lyons and sentenced him to life in prison.

Marshall appealed the Lyons case all the way to the United States Supreme Court, arguing that the trial judge erred by admitting into evidence the confession of a defendant who had been beaten and held without food or water for nearly 24 hours. When the Supreme Court refused to overturn the conviction, *The Black Dispatch* called the decision dangerous. "If left to stand it means citizens regardless of color may be inhumanely clubbed in the morning. . . which will make it entirely legal to in such manner extort confessions from those held in jail and under arrest."[4] It was Marshall's first defeat in a case before the United States Supreme Court, in fact his first defeat in a major decision involving the rights of a black defendant.

Marshall later reflected that he never lost faith in human nature, even after facing the scowling courtroom spectators in Hugo. He wrote, "Even in the most prejudiced communities, the majority of the people have some respect for truth and some sense of justice, no matter how deeply hidden it is at times."[5]

Some legal scholars agree that Marshall's argument in the Lyons case led later courts to place stringent requirements on law enforcement agencies in their treatment of suspects placed under arrest.

"Jimmy Says" continued to be a widely read column in *The Black Dispatch* in the early 1940s. Stewart covered every social or civic event in town and wrote about them with a flair, "Really saw a swell affair last week. Went out to the Country Club to help old Red Adkins at the Betty Slick reception. Never in these years have

I seen anything to compared with the elaborate decorations and delicious, refreshing food and drink that those people had. Again I found cause to laugh at segregation. . . There they were, spending thousands of dollars to stage the affair. They paid us to serve them but didn't feel any of us their equal, yet we saw, heard and just about got as much kick out of the reception as they did excepting, the dressing, and to tell the truth, I'll bet we were more comfortable in our jackets than any of them were in their tuxedos." [6]

Stewart supplemented his ONG income by working as a waiter at parties thrown by wealthy families. He later recalled that some of the families must have considered him "deaf and dumb" because they talked about things that "surely they did not want repeated."

Stewart improved his writing skills by completing a correspondence course in journalism from the Newspaper Institute. His tuition was paid by the G.I. Bill.

Oklahoma Natural Gas approved of the way Stewart performed his job as manager of the eastside office. The company was especially proud of the publicity Stewart received from his newspaper column so supervisors never cared if Stewart left early to cover a civic event.

Stewart often tried his hand at sports writing for *The Black Dispatch*. Even in covering a football game, Stewart found an opportunity to speak out for blacks: "The color line will be broken sometimes in sports. Color lines mean nothing to our kids. They play in the north as much as in the south. Matter of fact, we'll play anybody who'll put the ball down anywhere."[7]

Stewart informed his readers about important events around town, "Douglass High is again host this week to the Invitational Speech Tournament. . . go by and hear what our youth are thinking and speaking about."[8]

Stewart had a certain flair about his writing when it came to describing a special event involving music on Second Street. After Christmas Eve of 1940, Stewart wrote:

Twas the night before Christmas, when all was astir. For speed, sport and frolic one didn't have to go far. The joints were all jumping. Ruby's Grill had most of the town's jitterbugs and did they swing. Ruby had to stop the orchestra to get them in good enough order to go back to the breakfast dance up at Slaughter's. . . After mass at one of the churches, the Sharp End got sharper. Came early morning and the breakfast danced with Wallace and his Wooly Cats. Everybody there seemed to have got their solid kicks from dark 'til broad daylight. These breakfast dances are the thing. . . Christmas Day, and a dead one until afternoon, for those cats that made the rounds that night. After a fill-o-food the stem is jumping again. Same old joints, just open for new business.[9]

Commentary on elections in *The Black Dispatch* was usually the job for editor Dunjee. But after all candidates favored by the black community lost in a city election in 1940, Stewart wrote, "Every shady character from the Canadian river bottoms to the State Capitol were rounded up and voted in the election Tuesday. . . Lots of us couldn't find time to see Jackie Robinson and vote too, so we let the voting go and went to the ball game." Robinson, who became major league baseball's first black player in 1947, was playing an exhibition game in Oklahoma City.

Stewart scolded his readers for not voting. "Citizenship is earned and not given, and none should know this better than the minorities. If we are ever to accept the rights and privileges of full citizenship, we must accept the duties and responsibilities that go along with it. There is an old proverb 'don't cry over spilled milk' and liberal causes as far as I can see will have another two year wait, but I see no justification for not tying the darn cow's leg before it happens again. Do you?"[10]

From the time Stewart assumed a leadership role in the local NAACP, he constantly championed issues in his quest for equality. In 1942 he urged his fellow citizens to encourage their children to take advantage of training programs administered by the National Youth Administration (NYA), one of the New Deal programs of the administration of President Franklin D. Roosevelt. "NYA welding, sheet metal, and wood work classes are going strong. . . Is your boy making plans to better fit himself for life? The defense classes at Douglass are in need of men. Sepias, let's not have it said that we don't want training after crying so long and loud for it."[11]

Nothing escaped Stewart's watchful eye. From week to week in his column, he asked city officials, "When will the city park department cut those weeds and high grass in our parks? We are Americans too," or "Colored bus drivers? That's not impossible. I've seen them training numerous drivers of other races on the East Fourth Street line lately. Sleep on Nero, Rome hasn't been burned yet." [12]

Stewart was 29 when the Japanese bombed Pearl Harbor on December 7, 1941, hurling the United States into World War II against the Axis powers of Germany, Japan, and Italy. Stewart used his weekly column to call for unity of purpose for all Americans in defeating the enemy. He joined Dunjee in appearances at local churches and at parks to honor young black men who were enlisting in or being drafted by the army to fight for freedom in Europe and the Pacific.

Stewart was concerned about the morale of black Oklahomans fighting in the war. He hosted USO shows for visiting servicemen. In his newspaper column, he wrote to Oklahoma GIs: "Boys in Army camps everywhere. Let me know your whereabouts, your friends would like to write you if they knew where to write."[13] Stewart also worked as a volunteer civilian recruiter and sent some of the first black recruits to the United States Marine Corps.

In 1942 Stewart fell in love with young Mae Lois Layne, whom he had met a few years earlier at Langston University. Mae Lois had been born September 9, 1917, in McAlester, Oklahoma, to Walter and Bernice Lois Layne. Walter and Bernice were only 17 when Mae Lois arrived, and their marriage ended soon after. Bernice married Willie A. Crawley, who officially adopted Mae Lois.

Mae Lois's mother, Bernice Lois Layne Crawley, had been born at Alderson in Indian Territory August 16, 1900. Her father was

Stewart was proud of his service in the United States Marine Corps. He spent his entire service time at Camp Lejeune, North Carolina, where he and Mae Lois brought their two children into the world.

H. E. "Zeke" Miller, one of the famous United States deputy marshals who patrolled Indian country for federal judge Isaac Parker in Fort Smith, Arkansas. Parker's court had federal jurisdiction over Indian Territory and Parker was known as the "hanging judge" for his sentencing of more than 100 convicted felons to death by hanging.

Mae Lois Layne and Stewart were married after a short courtship on May 12, 1942. In October of that year Stewart organized an army relief football game to raise money to furnish recreation rooms for black soldiers stationed at the Midwest Air Depot in Oklahoma City. Stewart enlisted the help of Langston University football coach "Zip" Gayles, separate schools director F.D. Moon, USO director Mary Holman, the NAACP, the Oklahoma City Negro Chamber of Commerce, and the James Europe Post 157 of the American Legion.

Stewart urged blacks in Oklahoma City to get behind the project, "Don't think for a moment that these rooms can be furnished for a song and dance. 'Twill take real cash, but I know you Okies will support the cause."[14]

One reason Stewart wanted the charity football game to be successful was the fact that he was awaiting assignment in the fighting forces of the United States, "Oklahoma people are war conscious. They know the government as such can't look after the every need of the armed forces; they have brothers, cousins, fathers, sisters and now mothers in or directly affected by the war. They're willing to help defend the greatest country every known to mankind and will support any worthwhile charity even if they have to walk to work a couple of days to do so. Knowing these fine Oklahomans as I do and knowing also that I only have short time to be among them, I wanted to be a part of a great movement of Oklahomans for the benefit of men in service so that when I'm far away I can stick my chest out and say, 'We got the job done back in Oklahoma.' "[15]

Stewart had volunteered for duty in the United States Marine Corps. For six months he was investigated because a recruiter had obtained copies of his columns in *The Black Dispatch* and labeled

Stewart as a troublemaker. Finally, the Marines accepted him. In February, 1943, Stewart was sent for basic training at Camp Lejeune, North Carolina. He and Mae Lois visited his mother in Wichita, Kansas for a few days and then boarded a Rock Island train in Oklahoma City for the trip to North Carolina.

Stewart continued to send "Jimmy Says" columns back to the newspaper in Oklahoma City. He wrote about his train ride to become a Marine: "The train is very crowded. Passengers sitting at every table in the diner as though it was meal time. Porter took my bags and assisted me to my berth, got up 30 minutes out of Memphis, Tennessee, almost missing seeing Arkansas."

Stewart told his readers about the slow train that he took from Hamlet, North Carolina to Wilmington:

Tis almost the same as a taxi for the farmers, sawmillers, tobacco workers, in this section. Nearly every section line has a name and a station and the people get on with everything from fried fish with hoecakes (large biscuits) to clothes bundles, chickens, and milk. One lady was assisted on just now with a bundle wrapped in a quilt and asked Sam, the train porter on this flying genny who knows about everyone who gets on, what he had done with her milk. He told her that the railroad was getting on him for letting them bring their livestock in the passenger coach, therefore he had placed her milk in the baggage car. Sam was the kind of porter that you see in the *Saturday Evening Post.* He sold Coca Cola and sandwiches all of the way.[17]

Stewart was assigned to the 51st Defense Battalion, the first black battalion in the Marine Corps. He found segregation and discrimination very much part of his life as a soldier, especially in North Carolina. He was proud of his Marine uniform and did not think he deserved whispered slurs from whites who did not believe blacks could, or should fight in the war. When Stewart complained of the discrimination to editor Dunjee back in Oklahoma City, Dunjee wrote in a scathing editorial, "Think of it! The army,

James Edward Stewart, Jr. was born May 14, 1944. Zandra Jean Stewart was born May 28, 1945. Stewart chose the name Sandra; the spelling that began with a "Z" was in honor of the child's great grandfather Zeke Miller.

controlled by Southerners, bars Negroes from most combat units, casts him into supply and engineer divisions, and then tells an astonished world the Negro cannot and will not fight. There is nothing in America more unholy and cowardly than the disposition of certain vicious elements in America to assert that black men are incapable of doing anything, and proving it by never letting them try. . . There is a trail of black blood that wends its way throughout American history. Black men have fought with white men for the perpetuity of American ideals. . . Many times the Negro has had to separate himself from the white man's hypocrisy to defend ideals that were dear to the hearth and fireside of the black man."[18]

The Stewart family grew while Jimmy and Mae Lois were at Camp Lejeune. After their first baby was stillborn, Mae Lois gave birth to James Edward Stewart, Jr. on May 14, 1944. A baby girl, Zandra Jean Stewart, followed on May 28, 1945. Stewart wanted to name the baby girl Sandra. The "Z" was added to her name in honor of Mae Lois's grandfather, "Zeke" Miller.

Stewart rose to the rank of Steward First Class, excelled on the Camp Lejeune post basketball team, and served honorably until he was discharged December 6, 1945, with mustering-out pay of $264.55 in his pocket. He was extremely proud of his Marine service and hardly ever appeared in public throughout his life without a Marine lapel pin or tie tac.

FIVE

EQUALITY IN THE CLASSROOM

STEWART returned to his job in Oklahoma City with ONG after he was discharged from the Marines. The company expected post-war growth in Oklahoma City and opened a second office on the eastside. Stewart was given additional staff members to help the growing demand for natural gas.

On civil rights issues, Stewart picked up where he left off before the war. Education and jobs for returning black veterans were the battlefields he chose for several significant campaigns in the years following the war. At the end of 1946 Stewart was re-elected president of the Oklahoma City Branch of the NAACP.

Stewart expected opposition to his civil rights advances in Oklahoma City. However, he was not prepared for the apathy of his own black neighbors. He said, "There will always be people who would rather be pleasant than free, and even those who have gained the most from our efforts sometimes don't realize where the help came from."[1]

One of Stewart's first projects was to confront federal post office officials who refused to hire blacks. Technically civil service jobs were open to minorities for several years before World War II, but Oklahoma City postal officials always said there were no permanent positions. Instead, they made only temporary appointments, and the assignments went only to whites.

Stewart failed in his attempts to talk to local officials about the problem. He was told by postmaster Fred Shaw that hiring blacks to deliver mail would create unrest in the community because "people weren't in the right frame of mind" to receive their mail from black mail carriers.

Stewart took his fight to Washington, D.C. and the newly created Veterans' Affairs Committee of the United States Civil Service Commission. Stewart spearheaded a massive letter-writing campaign which resulted in the opening of the Civil Service rolls to blacks. The strategy worked. Within months, blacks qualified and were hired as postal employees.[2]

Stewart also was passionate about equal educational opportunities for black students. He helped launch a frontal attack on prejudice and the open and obvious inequality of separate schools for black children in Oklahoma, a cruel form of discrimination that had existed since before statehood.

Segregation was not always a divisive issue in Oklahoma. After Oklahoma Territory was organized in 1890 the territorial legislature left segregation up to local voters. Each April counties were allowed to vote whether or not to have separate schools for black children. Even laws establishing the University of Oklahoma, the Agricultural and Mechanical College at Stillwater, and the Normal School at Edmond did not prohibit the admission of blacks.

However, with the territorial legislature's exclusion of black children in elementary and secondary schools in 1897, the idea of "separate but equal" schools became embedded into the fabric of Oklahoma's educational system as it was throughout the South. At statehood, Oklahoma's constitution provided that "separate schools for white and colored with like accommodations" would be funded by the legislature.

Historian Jimmie Lewis Franklin has written that, "Whites regarded separate schools as an important cornerstone of Oklahoma's segregated society. Although whites spoke of 'separate but equal' schools, few blacks believed. . . Very simply, the state devised a plan which produced fewer dollars for black schools than for white ones."[3]

Franklin recognized that segregated schools supported the social system built by whites. "The schools, then, became a powerful instrument in the caste system, for they actively served as an effective counterweight to any idea of assimilation." 4

Money, or the lack thereof, made it impossible for separate schools to be equal schools, with equal educational opportunities for black and white children alike. A complex school financing system perpetuated inferior schools for blacks in Oklahoma for decades after statehood. Black schools were financed with a county-wide tax levy. White schools, however, received both county tax money and money from a school district property tax levy. Whites owned most of the property and white schools received the great bulk of tax money earmarked for education. In some years, during the fight for school equality, white schools received five times as much as black schools. *The Black Dispatch* called Oklahoma's school laws "perhaps the most indefensible and reprehensible in the nation."5

Discrimination in funding was not easy to hide. In 1919, 12 years after statehood, the average expenditure for white students was $22.60, almost twice the $11.50 per black student expenditure. Two decades later, when Stewart and Roscoe Dunjee turned up the heat in the fight for equal education for black children, funding for black schools had not appreciably improved. Dunjee wrote, "The whole sorry mess pukes up the utter rottenness of separate schools. Education conditions will never be ideal until separate schools have been abolished."6

A special problem was the lack of funding for capital improvements for black school districts. White officials often authorized an additional tax levy for capital projects but county voters simply did not approve the levy on election day. Poor and unhealthy facilities for black students resulted from the lack of capital improvement spending.

Stewart sought advice on the equality in education issue from F. D. Moon, a pioneer black educator who was born in 1896 in Fallis, Oklahoma. Moon, a graduate of Langston University, became president of the Oklahoma Association of Negro Teachers (OANT) in 1929 and guided that organization through a series of campaigns to improve funding for schools, and teachers. He became a legend as principal of Douglass High School, beginning his term as head of the state's largest black school in 1941.

Moon knew the problems of inadequate funding for black schools firsthand. His first principal's job was in the small town of Crescent. Like most rural black schools, Crescent had insufficient funds for staff and maintenance of its dilapidated buildings. Moon was determined to improve the funding of black schools and spent much of his time studying the problem.

In 1946 Moon asked Stewart and the NAACP for help in passing an amendment to Oklahoma's constitution that would increase the building tax levy available to black districts. Stewart and the NAACP responded to Moon's request and raised money to promote the successful campaign to adopt the constitutional amendment.

For the first time, Stewart was on the opposite side of an issue with his mentor, editor Roscoe Dunjee, who was convinced that "Negro educators were probably sold down the river." Dunjee believed that the legislature should change the school law periodically rather than amend the constitution to simply authorize a vote on an additional tax levy. Dunjee was convinced that most white voters still would not approve an additional tax, even if it was constitutionally permitted.

In the general election on November 5, 1946, Oklahoma voters approved the constitutional amendment. The additional one mil levy could be used only for the acquisition of property and the erection of buildings for separate schools for white and black children.

Black teachers suffered financially because of the separate school financing scheme. There was a large gap between salaries for white and black teachers. In 1943 Oklahoma City School Superintendent H. E. Wrinkle reported that the average annual salary for white teachers was $1,640.92 while the average salary of black teachers was $1,347.66, a difference of almost $300 a year.[7]

The issue of inequality of pay for black teachers came to a head in April, 1947, when Stewart and others convinced a brilliant

Douglass High School physical education teacher, Emma Lee Freeman, to bring a lawsuit against the Oklahoma City Board of Education to force equal pay. Freeman, a 12-year veteran public school teacher, was a graduate of Kansas State Teachers' College.

Freeman was represented by Tulsa attorney Amos T. Hall, a legal champion for the poor and oppressed of Oklahoma. Hall, a Louisiana native, began practicing law in Tulsa in 1925 and was at the forefront of Oklahoma civil rights legal battles for 30 years, representing the NAACP in its most famous victories. He later was the first black to be elected to a county-wide office and the first black man to be elected associate district judge in Oklahoma.

In Freeman's lawsuit, Hall argued that she had the same qualifications and same experience and did the same work as her white counterparts in Oklahoma City. The only difference was that Freeman was paid a salary that was substantially less than white teachers.

A petition for declaratory judgment was filed in the United States District Court for the Western District of Oklahoma. The federal court was simply asked to declare the unequal pay system in violation of the Fourteenth Amendment to the United States Constitution which guaranteed equal protection for all citizens.

After the lawsuit was filed, School Board Vice President Ira Williams told reporters he was surprised by the action, "We have tried to make salaries equal, but sometimes there is nothing we can do about it." [8]

Freeman's case was dismissed after pay scales were equalized. However, Stewart and the NAACP, through its attorney, pushed for a federal court ruling that would guide school boards in pay controversies. *The Black Dispatch* editorialized, "The Emma Lee Freeman salary differential suit should be continued in federal court, despite the recent arrangement by which Oklahoma City Negro teachers received their salaries as per contract. To stop short on compromise and not secure a declaratory judgment would be extremely short-sighted. We want to urge that the NAACP continue this case so that it will be obligatory that county government provide Negro teachers the same salaries paid whites." [9]

In October, 1948, United States District Judge Edgar S. Vaught handed down a ruling that Stewart, F. D. Moon, and black teachers everywhere had been waiting for. Vaught ordered all school boards in the state to give black and white teachers equal pay. The court order cut right to the heart of the matter, "It is unlawful under the 14th Amendment. . . for any of the defendants to discriminate as to salaries between teachers in the majority schools and teachers in the separate schools on account of race." [10]

Stewart saw another problem in educating black children, the education of students' parents as to the importance of education. He recognized that whole families of blacks left their homes to pick cotton in the fall, taking their kids out of school in the process. Stewart later wrote, "It was nothing to see big, strapling six-footers in the fourth or fifth grades. . . In those days the kids were flunked and held back. . . Parents who held their children out for work or other reasons caused them to lag and a large percent dropped out rather than stay in school where in many instances they were older than the teachers, as well as larger." [11]

Stewart and the NAACP petitioned the board of education for a black truant officer to help keep black children in school. During Negro History and Negro Health weeks, Stewart put together groups of volunteers to contact parents with the message that education was a sure-fire method to escape poverty and find decent, good-paying jobs upon graduation.

Stewart always worked coolly under pressure. He seldom raised his voice or lost his temper, even when white opponents called him everything but human and when the white school superintendent told Stewart he was "getting in his hair" too much. Stewart's civil methods won him friends in the white community. Thousands of sympathetic whites joined the movement for the abolition of separate schools. The equal education train was on the track, and would not be derailed.

Stewart never intended to be in the limelight in civil rights battles. He was comfortable in leading from the shadows and sharing credit with others in the fight. When the Oklahoma City Urban League was recognized by the National Urban League in November, 1946, Stewart was the first to applaud the formation of the new social welfare organization chapter in Oklahoma City. His first loyalty was to equality for his people, not to any particular organization, even though he served longer than anyone in history as president of the Oklahoma City Branch of the NAACP.

The Urban League was the nation's oldest social welfare group, founded in 1910. By 1946 when the Oklahoma City chapter was recognized, the National Urban League had local groups active in 56 American cities.

In 1947, Stewart wrote Urban League of Oklahoma City president Jesse T. Owens with congratulations on the Urban League's first anniversary: "Oklahoma City had need for, and is a better place in which to live, as a result of the Urban League's program of sound and constructive inter-racial teamwork through which intelligent social planning and action can be developed." [12]

Stewart's closest friends knew that one of his strongest leadership skills was his ability to get along with leaders of other organizations who were striving for the same goals. Stewart's files, which contain a half century of correspondence, reflect his cooperative feeling toward such organizations as the Oklahoma Social Welfare Association, Negro Chamber of Commerce, Council of Social Welfare, Oklahoma City Council of Churches, National Conference of Christians and Jews, Young Men's Christian Association, City Federation of Colored Women's Clubs, and the Urban League.

In 1947 the South, especially in North and South Carolina, was plagued with a series of horrendous crimes against blacks. Mobs lynched suspects on a weekly basis, denying them a fair trial

Frustrated that Congress and President Harry Truman apparently could not stop the lynchings, Stewart and Roscoe Dunjee began an educational program in *The Black Dispatch* and on local radio stations. The newspaper called on the president to issue a warning to the South that lynchings would not be tolerated, "What this nation needs today is a leader with towering moral courage. Lincoln freed the slaves as a war measure, and today we need a strong, virile leader who will visit his wrath upon these who spread disunity and discord through denial of constitutional rights to citizens."13

Stewart and Dunjee participated in 15-minute programs aired as a public service program by Oklahoma City radio stations. The program began with a brisk, up-beat version of the "Battle Hymn of the Republic." As the strains of "His truth is marching on" faded, Stewart began the program, "Good evening Mr. Dunjee. It seems that the acquittal of the defendants in that Greenville, South Carolina lynching case has touched off another series of lynchings throughout the United States."14

Dunjee then asked Stewart, as president of the local branch of the NAACP, how the organization felt about lynchings. Stewart held nothing back in his attack on lynchings:

> Naturally, we in the NAACP, as law-abiding citizens, are
> appalled that the states cannot guarantee a man a fair trial. The
> crime of lynching is affecting the position of the United States
> in its dealing with other nations. Lynching has become an
> international disgrace and something must be done about
> it. . . An atmosphere of suspicion and resentment in a country
> over the way a minority is being treated in the United States is
> a formidable obstacle to the development of mutual
> understanding and trust between the two countries.15

In the late 1940s Stewart saw the fall of many barriers that kept blacks from good jobs and adequate housing. However, discrimination was still alive and cruel in Oklahoma. When Stewart tried to help a young black man, Roger L. Davis, enroll for aviation training at Tulsa's Spartan School of Aeronautics, the rejection letter drilled home just how much discrimination was still present.

Spartan Vice President Maxwell Balfour wrote, "We have little or no demand for training from people of your race and, therefore, have never made any provisions to care for them. I do know that there are schools in the Northeast portion of the country where people of color are accepted. I would suggest that you consult the aviation magazines and write to some of those schools."16

In 1947 Stewart represented the NAACP on a city-wide committee to raise money to build two new centers for the Young Men's Christian Association (YMCA), one center for whites and one for blacks. *The Daily Oklahoman* publisher E. K. Gaylord was chairman of the committee that raised $1,250,000 for the new YMCA for whites and $250,000 for a new building for blacks. In July, 1949, eight lots in the 600 block of Northeast Fourth Street were purchased. A building committee, headed by Dr. W. H. Slaughter, planned and monitored construction of the black YMCA.

From his first years as president of the Oklahoma City Branch of the NAACP, Stewart was active in the national NAACP organization. Dunjee was on the national board of directors and used his influence to obtain Stewart's appointment to various committees. In 1947 Stewart was instrumental in developing a plan to regionalize the operations of the NAACP. From the organization's inception, all activities were controlled from the headquarters in New York City. Stewart and other leaders drafted, and the national board of directors approved, a plan to establish regional offices.

Oklahoma was part of the Southwest Region which officially opened its office in Dallas, Texas, on November 1, 1948. A lawyer was assigned to each region to monitor legal battles. Stewart was immediately elected to the regional board of directors for the Southwest Region.

Stewart attended the 1949 national NAACP convention and was appointed chairman of the Committee on Time and Place, its job to select a site for the 1950 national meeting. Stewart traveled to Boston, Massachusetts and Atlanta, Georgia, two cities which expressed an interest in hosting the 1950 convention. Stewart worked closely with committee co-chairman Dr. W. R. Laney of Rock Hill, South Carolina, and Secretary Ollie Mae Weeks of Indianapolis, Indiana. After visits to Boston and Atlanta, Boston was chosen as the site for the convention.

In the 1940s Stewart had the good fortune to work with two legendary leaders of the NAACP, Walter White and Roy Wilkins. Walter Francis White was a Georgia native who joined the

NAACP staff in New York City in 1918. In 1931 White became the executive director of the NAACP and forged an unprecedented alliance among church, ethnic, labor, civil liberties, and women's organizations that were crucial to the success of the civil rights movement in the 1960s. White directed the efforts of the NAACP until his death in 1955.[17]

Roy Ottaway Wilkins was born the son of a Methodist minister in Missouri. In 1931 he was hired by Walter White as assistant executive director of the NAACP. He succeeded W. E. B. Du Bois as editor of *The Crisis,* the official magazine of the NAACP, in 1935. When White died in 1955, Wilkins became executive secretary of the NAACP. He led the organization during its finest hour, during the major civil rights battles of the 1950s and 60s. He retired in 1977 and died five years later.[18]

Stewart looked up to four men in America. They were Roscoe Dunjee, Walter White, Roy Wilkins, and Thurgood Marshall.

SIX

ADA LOIS SIPUEL FISHER

D IFFICULT AND PROTRACTED are two words which adequately describe the battle of Stewart, Roscoe Dunjee, Thurgood Marshall, the NAACP, and a cast of hundreds to desegregate Oklahoma's institutions of higher education in the 1940s.

Delegates from 86 local branches of the NAACP in Oklahoma met in McAlester for their annual meeting in November, 1945. More than 200 delegates approved a course of action that would shake the very foundation of segregation in American higher education and set off a storm of controversy over the rights of blacks to attend state-run universities.

Dunjee, the state president of the Oklahoma Conference of Branches, and Stewart invited NAACP chief legal counsel Marshall to McAlester to discuss ways and means to break the hold of segregation.

The decision was made to test Oklahoma's segregation laws by supporting black students who planned to enroll at both the University of Oklahoma and Oklahoma A&M University. News accounts of the NAACP decision created panic among leaders of higher education. The University of Oklahoma Board of Regents met and voted unanimously to deny admission to "anyone of the Negro blood."[1]

Seven years earlier, the United States Supreme Court, in the case of *Missouri ex rel. Gaines v. Canada,* had ruled that a black student, Lloyd Gaines, either be admitted to the University of Missouri law school or that a separate school be set up for blacks in Missouri. Oklahoma's official response to the *Gaines* decision was to appropriate funds for black students who were forced to leave the state to enroll in courses not offered at all-black Langston University, even though Gaines stood for the proposition that "equality in education must occur within the state."[2]

In 1945, any unbiased observer could easily conclude that higher education in Oklahoma was separate, but certainly not equal. The printing plant at OU had a worldwide reputation for excellence while the printing equipment at Langston was so outdated that editor Dunjee used his own presses at *The Black Dispatch* to print the school's class catalogues. Dunjee called Langston "a worthless educational makeshift," and accused segregationists of "putting a steeple on a honky tonk," when Langston was held up as an example of equal higher education for blacks in Oklahoma.[3]

By January, 1946, the stage was set for a legal battle that would pit a young black girl from Chickasha, Oklahoma, against the institution of segregation in America, a battle that would reverberate from sea to shining sea.

Stewart, Dunjee, and Dr. W. A. J. Bullock, a Chickasha physician and longtime civil rights advocate, met in early January to plan Ada Lois Sipuel Fisher's enrollment in the OU School of Law. Fisher had graduated with honors from Langston University and was carefully selected by the NAACP as the right person to test Oklahoma's oppressive segregation laws.

On January 14, Dunjee and Dr. Bullock accompanied Fisher to the office of OU president Dr. George L. Cross. Cross was sympathetic with Fisher's plight, but told the young black student that his hands were tied and he could not admit her. Dunjee asked Cross for a letter stating that the only reason for denying Fisher admission was her race. Cross complied with the request. The court battle was about to begin.

Stewart and Dunjee launched a massive fund raising effort to finance what was expected to be a long and costly legal battle. Contributions from local branches of the NAACP, churches, and individuals began to flow. Stewart and Dunjee appeared with Fisher at mass meetings at churches, schools, bingo halls, and cafes.

Fisher later wrote, "We developed a regular pattern, a kind of road show that we presented...Wherever two or three African Americans might gather, there we were also."[4]

Eventually the Fisher road show consisted of Fisher, Dunjee, Stewart, Professor Melvin Tolson of Langston University, and Dr. William Boyd of El Reno, the state treasurer of the NAACP. Fisher explained, "We often rode with Dr. Boyd, who had a new car and was a good, safe driver. Dr. Tolson expounded away on literature, politics... From time to time, Dunjee would interrupt with a joke."[5]

Somehow the money necessary to fund Fisher's legal battle came in. There were no corporate contributors, just common people giving nickels and dimes. The community of Bristow, Oklahoma, gave $2.15, the Landmark Baptist Church chipped in $1.40. Miraculously, thousands of dollars were raised.

The strategy sessions for Fisher's legal challenge were held at the office of *The Black Dispatch*. In her autobiography, *A Matter of Black and White,* Fisher recalled her first meeting with Stewart, Dunjee, attorney Amos T. Hall, and her lead lawyer, the famous Thurgood Marshall:

> I was a bit nervous about meeting the famous barrister
> [Marshall]. I spoke to everyone, and then Dunjee told Marshall,
> "This is the young lady." Thurgood immediately put me at ease
> by standing up, shaking my hand, and then giving me a big,
> friendly hug. We were strangers no more.[6]

Fisher was in awe of Marshall, who had "encountered the Ku Klux Klan, the White Knights, and every variety of hate and racist groups." Marshall, the perennial storyteller, entertained Fisher, Stewart and Dunjee at lunch after the strategy meeting with stories of his many arrests and scuffles fighting for civil rights in the South.

Dunjee went on the attack in his weekly newspaper writing, "The young black girl has the same right to effectively utilize her next six years just as girls of any other race... Separate schools are focal in the idea that one human being is better than another, and we shall always oppose them. . . Separate schools are intended to chain black folk within the confines of inferiority." [8]

The Fisher lawsuit was filed in Cleveland County on May 6, 1946. Stewart sat on the front row at the initial hearing in the case July 9. The Cleveland County Courthouse was not yet air-conditioned. The hot and steamy July Oklahoma day was topped only by the hot and intense rhetoric of Fisher's lawyers.

As expected, the local district judge and the Oklahoma Supreme Court both upheld Oklahoma's segregation law. The adverse rulings did not discourage Stewart, Fisher, Marshall, or the legal team Marshall had put together for the battle, including Amos T. Hall, University of Illinois professor Robert Ming, and James Nabritt, dean of the law school at Howard University.

Marshall took Fisher's case to the United States Supreme Court which, in January, 1948, reversed the Oklahoma decisions and ordered the state to provide Fisher with a legal education in a state school. However, it was only a limited victory for Fisher. The nation's highest court still did not strike down the laws that allowed segregated facilities in higher education.

Oklahoma authorities quickly moved to again deny Fisher's admission. Under order of the Supreme Court to provide Fisher with a legal education, the state established the "Langston University School of Law," a hastily improvised sham law school with three faculty members. Fisher, upon advice of her attorneys, refused to enter the Langston law school. When the Langston law school closed in the summer of 1949 Fisher was allowed to enroll in the University of Oklahoma School of Law. She graduated in 1951 and began a long and distinguished career as an educator and civil rights activist.

Stewart met with attorney Marshall in New York in early 1948 to map plans for continuing the desegregation battle. Armed with courage and hope from the Fisher decision in the United States Supreme Court, the NAACP broadened its attack. Stewart encouraged six black students to apply for admission to the University of Oklahoma to take courses not available at Langston.

The State Regents for Higher Education were in a tizzy. They had been ordered to provide equal opportunities for black students. Education officials wondered where the extra money would come from to provide separate, equal classes. A committee of deans from OU and Oklahoma A&M concluded that it would take $12 million to establish graduate departments at Langston. Stewart was not surprised, however, when OU defied all logic and denied admission to the six black students.

At the same time the six Oklahoma City students were attempting to enroll at OU, George W. McLaurin, a 54-year-old Langston University instructor, applied for admission to the graduate school at OU. In September, 1948, a three-judge federal district court panel ordered Oklahoma to admit McLaurin.

Ada Lois Sipuel Fisher, right, discusses legal tactics with her world-class lawyers Amos T. Hall, left, of Tulsa and Thurgood Marshall, who later became the first black to serve on the United States Supreme Court. (Courtesy *The Daily Oklahoman*.)

Still, Oklahoma balked, refusing to abandon its policy of segregation. The legislature passed a statute to permit the admission of blacks in state schools where courses were not available at Langston. Tragically the legislation required that the courses be given to blacks on a segregated basis.

On the first day of class, OU officials placed McLaurin's desk in an alcove in the classroom where he could see the teacher and the teacher could see him, but McLaurin could not see his fellow students. All of McLaurin's classes were held in the same room in the Carnegie Building on the Norman campus. Thurgood Marshall called the move "stupid."

Burdened with the details of special requests for special courses and programs, higher education officials gave up their fight in late 1949 and asked the legislature to permit the wholesale enrollment of black students. No doubt the Fisher and McLaurin decisions struck a body blow at the principle of segregation in America's schools.

The Fisher and McLaurin case started the unraveling of Oklahoma's segregation statutes but there was still much to be done. Stewart was forced to take the lead in the desegregation fight because Dunjee's health was failing, prompting his resignation as statewide president of the NAACP, a position he held for 20 years. Dunjee's resignation at the 1949 Oklahoma NAACP convention shocked black Oklahomans. Stewart read the president's annual message, reviewing the landmark victories won by the NAACP during the year. When Stewart announced Dunjee's decision to step down, there was "shocked silence, then murmurs of surprise, and finally tears."[9]

Stewart, never one to stand out front to take the credit, stood with tears in his eyes at a giant celebration in honor of Ada Lois Fisher's graduation from law school in 1951. The NAACP sponsored the event at the Calvary Baptist Church in Oklahoma City. At the close of the service, Fisher embraced Dunjee and Stewart and thanked them for making a difference in her life and the lives of all black Americans.

SEVEN

A NEW BLACK
HIGH SCHOOL

IN THE LATE 1940S Stewart was at the forefront of the movement in the Oklahoma City black community to promote the construction of a new black high school. Douglass High School, located at 600 North High Street, was terribly overcrowded. Nearly 1,500 students were housed in buildings that could reasonably accommodate only 950.

The junior high school band was forced to meet in a hallway, creating unacceptable learning conditions for band members or nearby students. *The Black Dispatch* reported, "This means that horns are continually being blown which serves as a distracting element for teachers who are trying to carry on physical education classes in the gymnasium." [1]

There were two reasons why Douglass High School was overcrowded. The black population of Oklahoma City had gradually increased since statehood and wartime babies' entrance into the school system created an unprecedented shortage of teachers and facilities.

The dream of a new black high school actually began in December, 1945, when Oklahoma County voters approved a $700,000 bond issue for black schools in the county. It was the first time in state history that Oklahoma County held a bond election to finance separate schools. Stewart, and his employer, Oklahoma Natural Gas Company, publicly backed the efforts to adequately fund both black and white schools.

Stewart, the NAACP, and the Negro Chamber of Commerce

worked hard to convince black voters to approve the bond issue which also provided $4,000,000 for majority white schools and millions more for roads and capital projects in Oklahoma County. Voters in the seven black precincts in northeast Oklahoma City overwhelmingly approved the bond issue, 1,060 to 18.

A portion of the 1945 bond money was used to build the state's first swimming pool for black children. Stewart was present in September, 1949, when Oklahoma City Mayor Allen Street dedicated the new $120,000 pool at Douglass High School.

The $700,000 bond issue floated in 1945 was inadequate to fully fund the purchase of land and the construction of a new black high school. Stewart and other leaders first considered locating the new high school on property occupied by Washington Park just north of the railroad tracks on Northeast Fourth Street. However, heavy opposition developed to that location and school officials looked elsewhere.

The Oklahoma City Board of Education allocated $380,000 to purchase 26 acres of land at the old Fair Park at Northeast Tenth Street and Eastern Avenue. Fair Park consisted of 160 acres that extended east from Eastern Avenue to the Katy Railroad tracks and from Northeast Fourth to Northeast Tenth Street.

In 1948 the board of education purchased 26 acres, the 4-H Club building, the FFA Building, the livestock pavilion, and several other smaller buildings at the old fairground site when the State Fair Board announced plans to move the State Fair to a new location at Northwest Tenth Street and May Avenue in northwest Oklahoma City.[2]

When progress on the new fairgrounds project stalled, more pressure was applied to the black community to pass another bond issue in 1950 to improve roads and sewers. The bonds were not designed to directly finance a new black high school. Instead, city leaders sought support from Stewart and the Negro Chamber of Commerce on the promise that more bond money could help move the fairgrounds and speed up the construction of the new school at Northeast Tenth and Eastern.

Stewart was named chairman of a Negro Chamber of Commerce committee to evaluate the impact of the May, 1950, bond election on the black community. Other committee members were Earl Miller, W. M. Taylor, F. D. Moon, W. C. Price, A. D. Mathues, John Simmons, and George Ragland.

Stewart and his committee met with the Oklahoma City Park Board and the Greater City Committee, a citizens group formed to promote the bond issue. City officials agreed to extend sewer service down Page Avenue from Northeast Sixteenth Street to Tenth Street to provide service for Edwards School. Stewart was able to obtain commitments from the leaders of the Greater City Committee to allocate some of the funds to move the fairgrounds, a project that Stewart knew must be completed before a new black high school could become a reality.[3]

On election day, black voters stamped their approval on the bond issue by a ten-to-one margin. Stewart and Douglass principal F. D. Moon used a growing Parent Teachers Association (PTA) at Douglass to educate potential voters about the benefits of the bond issue package. Ruby Hall was a leader of the Douglass PTA that grew to membership of more than 300 parents by late 1950. Radio stations KLPR and KBYE, *The Black Dispatch*, and the Aldridge and Jewel theaters pitched in to promote membership in the Douglass PTA.

F. D. Moon realized in 1950 that still another bond issue would be needed to meet the expanded budget for constructing a high school facility to allow quality education for the nearly 1,500 students at Douglass. Moon called upon Stewart, the NAACP, the Negro Chamber of Commerce, and the Douglass PTA to petition school and city officials to submit a new bond issue to voters. The one-mill building levy available to black schools simply did not generate enough annual income to raise an additional $150,000 Moon felt he needed to build the new school plant. Moon was concerned that if he had to wait on a new school until he accumulated the $150,000, "it will be done at a terrific cost to education for black youth."[4]

Negro Chamber of Commerce President A. D. Mathues appointed F. D. Moon to chair a special committee of Stewart, Ira

D. Hall, George Ragland, Roscoe Dunjee, and Mrs. Cernoria D. Johnson to negotiate with city and school leaders.

On October 1, 1951, Stewart and the Negro Citizens' Committee presented a plan for a $1,500,000 bond issue to the Oklahoma City Board of Education. In a letter to the school board, the group asked for "speedy relief" since "an emergency exists in the consequence of the terrible overcrowded situation at Douglass." The board of education unanimously agreed with the citizens committee and passed a resolution calling on the Board of County Commissioners to include the school bond proposal in a $7 million county-wide bond election.

Stewart and Principal Moon received unexpected assistance from the League of Women Voters of Oklahoma County and the Federal Council of Church Women in gathering sufficient signatures to convince the county commissioners to call a special bond election. *The Daily Oklahoman* editorialized in favor of the new black high school:

> The additional building is needed badly. . . Up until recently, the facilities at the present high school for Negroes were adequate. But they are adequate no longer. The Negro population has grown exactly as the white population has grown. An additional high school building for Negroes is sorely needed and it should be built. The city is able to build it. It is the duty of the city to build it.[6]

It was so hot in Oklahoma City the summer the new black high school was built, bricks had to be cooled off before laid by a brickmason. (Courtesy *The Daily Oklahoman.*)

Ground was broken for the new black high school in ceremonies January 7, 1953. From left to right: C. B. McCray, president of the Oklahoma City Board of Education, Mrs. Cernoria Johnson, secretary of the Citizens Action Committee, and Douglass High School Principal F. D. Moon. (Courtesy *The Daily Oklahoman.*)

When white leaders balked at putting the school question on the ballot, Stewart and other black leaders threatened to attempt integration of Oklahoma City schools unless the new black high school was built. A group of 35 black citizens, including Stewart, met with county commissioners and presented a resolution that stated their intentions implicitly, "Therefore, if it [the construction of the new school] cannot be done now that we take immediate steps toward securing the admission of Negro youth to the junior high schools of Oklahoma City and the admission of senior

The old fairgrounds stadium was bricked in to provide additional space for industrial and vocational classrooms at the new Douglass High School. (Courtesy *The Daily Oklahoman*.)

high school youths to senior high schools carrying courses not offered at Douglass High School."[7]

After a closed-door session, county commissioners informally agreed to include a school bond section in the county-wide bond election. However, commissioners would not agree to allocate more than $900,000 of a $7,527,000 bond issue to be presented to Oklahoma County voters. Reverend W. K. Jackson, speaking for a newly-organized citizens committee, criticized the commissioners for arbitrarily cutting the amount of bond money that might be available for the construction of the new black high school.

Representatives of 32 black civic, social, and fraternity organizations attended a November 6 meeting of the Negro Citizens' Committee at St. John's Baptist Church to discuss the pros and cons of the proposed bond issue. Two major options were presented at the meeting. Blacks could either support the $900,000 bond issue and attempt to get the balance of construction money from other sources, or immediately proceed with integration efforts. Stewart and editor Dunjee told the group that regardless of whether or not the bond issue passed, the NAACP was moving ahead with its project to place black students in white schools.[8]

After heated debate, the Negro Citizens' Committee agreed to support the entire bond issue, including the $900,000 for the new black high school. Behind the scenes, Stanley Draper, manager of the Oklahoma City Chamber of Commerce, assured blacks that the board of education could find another $100,000 to complete the school project.

To successfully promote the county-wide bond issue, a committee was formed of leaders from both the black and white communities. Negro Chamber of Commerce president A. D. Mathues, Urban Road Bond Committee chairman Phil Daugherty, F. D. Moon, George Ragland, Stewart, and Reverend W. K. Jackson were appointed to the committee.

On December 5, six days before the election, Stewart addressed voters on a special program on KLPR Radio. He told listeners "Every man owes his community a service in return for the privilege of living in it... The bond issue election for better roads and schools is your chance as good citizens to make a payment on this account. You will never be able to pay it off in full."[9]

Stewart closed his radio address with a whole-hearted endorsement of the bond issue:

The road and school program paves the way for providing some of the essential things that large numbers of people, massed together, must have, and it prepares the facilities by which Oklahoma City's values may be displayed, not only to the people of Oklahoma, but to the whole world, to the end that more population, more industries, more jobs and better schooling will be available to all.[10]

The election was held December 11, 1951. Voters overwhelmingly approved the entire bond issue, including voting 21,386 to 4,767 for the separate high school issue.

It took six months for school and city officials and the State Fair Association's Board of Directors to finalize a land swap to make it possible for the State Fair to vacate the Northeast Tenth and Eastern property to make way for a new Douglass High

School. In May, 1952, the City Council put its stamp of approval on the tangled web of bond financing and land-swapping. Oklahoma City kept 120 acres of the old fairgrounds property to develop a black community center. City fathers also retained the newly constructed stone dairy barn to be used as a shop for the city park department.

Ground was broken for the new black high school in a lavish ceremony on the afternoon of January 7, 1953. Nearly 2,000 people attended the event that blacks had waited patiently a long time for. Stewart represented the NAACP as he sank one of the gold shovels into the dirt. The first shovel of dirt was turned by Mayor Allen Street. Joining the mayor and Stewart on the platform were A. D. Mathues; F. D. Moon; John C. Pearson, president of the school board; school superintendent J. Chester Swanson; Maude Brockway, president of the City Federation of Colored Women; and Reverend W. K. Jackson, the principal speaker for the celebration. Jackson told the audience, "This is an hour of destiny... We are beginning to erect an institution which will shape the lives of our citizenry."[11]

Incredibly, even more money was needed to complete the new Douglass High School. In 1953 Oklahoma County commissioners submitted another separate school bond issue. Voters once again approved the expenditure of the additional money necessary to complete the high school project.

The new high school opened in September, 1954. F. D. Moon introduced his 43 teachers and spoke of "The Land of Beginning Again," stressing everything from the kind of music he expected in the cafeteria to his insistence that students call teachers by their last names. Moon challenged the students, "Do you deserve this? Not unless you keep it and see that we turn over a new leaf in the care of it. Will you mar its beauty and show you are unworthy of beautification planned?"[12]

School Superintendent J. Chester Swanson presided over the dedication of the new high school May 1, 1955. Swanson told an audience of more than 2,000, "In the pleasure and pride of its reality we should not fail to recognize and accept the responsibility it entails, a responsibility to continue cooperatively, to effectively use these facilities for the betterment of mankind."[13]

The keynote speaker for the school dedication was Benjamin Mays, President of Morehouse College in Atlanta, Georgia, who applauded the efforts of the Negro Citizens' Committee in pushing the new school construction, "If a man is not willing to make a move for better conditions, he should not have them... The two races have been drawn closer together in working for the new high school than if you'd talked about it a thousand years and done nothing."[14]

When the new black high school was occupied, Stewart and other black civic leaders successfully campaigned to rename the old Douglass Junior-Senior High School the F. D. Moon Junior High School.

With the financial and political wrangling behind them, the Oklahoma City black community finally had a quality high school facility for its young men and women.

EIGHT
I AM PERSUADED

BY 1950, Stewart had led the Oklahoma City Branch of the NAACP during some of the most critical years of the organization's struggle for civil rights in America.

Stewart was a proud man. He was proud of his country, his color, his family, his city, and his God. Stewart was a faithful member of the Episcopal Church of the Redeemer. He filled his pew almost every Sunday and wholeheartedly supported church programs.

Stewart often used a quotation from the Bible, from the Apostle Paul, when talking about the fight for equality. Paul wrote to the Romans, "I am persuaded."[1] When appearing before civil and social clubs, Stewart said, "I am persuaded that God will allow me to live long enough to see my children treated equally with white kids and kids of every color." [2]

Stewart was not always completely optimistic about the future of the civil rights movement. Doubt flooded his mind some nights as he faced seemingly insurmountable problems in dealing with the latest crisis. However, by morning, Stewart always thought the problem through, weighed the circumstances of his action or inaction, and went on with life.

One of the most important and interesting fibers of Stewart's character was his integrity in relationships with both enemies and allies. When faced with a leadership dilemma, Stewart decided a course of action in his mind by asking himself a simple question, "What is the right thing to do?" Not, "What is best politically?" or

"What is the popular move to make?" but "What is the best for my people, for my city, for the cause of equality?" Later in life Stewart reflected that the decisions he based upon the simple question of what was right always turned out to be the right decisions.

Stewart was successful as a leader largely because of his ability to work with almost anyone, regardless of religion, color, or political belief. He never backed down from what he believed, but stood his ground in a manner which commanded respect from his followers and his detractors.

Under Stewart's leadership the NAACP in Oklahoma City was one of the most influential local branches of the national organization. The NAACP won a legion of major civil rights legal battles by the end of World War II. However, the organization's leadership recognized that the push for equality for all Americans was moving too slowly.

After the war the mood of national and local NAACP leaders changed, from goals of trying to influence society legislatively and judicially, to mobilizing minorities to actively demonstrate to further civil rights. The battle moved from the courthouse to the streets.

The Oklahoma City Branch of the NAACP was always respected in the community. But, under the smooth leadership of Stewart who served as president from 1946 to 1959, the branch became a powerful influence in Oklahoma City and state politics.

As the middle of the century approached, Stewart changed his mind about how to accomplish equality. He had been satisfied with fighting legal and political battles to further civil rights. Sometimes it was a lonely job. Sometimes it was an unpopular job. Oklahoma Natural Gas Company often received complaints from individuals and companies about Stewart's activities in the NAACP. Many Oklahomans urged the company to fire Stewart for what they considered to be ultra-liberal ideas. One anonymous, hand-written note arrived at the ONG office:

NIGGER LOVER YOU CANT FIGHT CITY HALL YOUR
TROUBLES ARE JUST STARTEN. FIRE HIM AND
YOU CAN STAY IN BUSSINESS IF YOU DONT
WATCH OUT

However, ONG supervisors knew Stewart's heart and his passion for equality. The company backed Stewart and even provided paper and mimeograph machines for circulars in bond issue and other politically-sensitive campaigns. ONG basically allowed Stewart to create his own time schedule managing the ONG Fourth Street office. He was free to leave the office any time he needed to work on projects to better northeast Oklahoma City.[3]

Stewart's new plan of action to work for civil rights was based upon the NAACP's ability to involve more people, lots of people, in its projects. Stewart believed that politicians paid attention to numbers and he could change votes on issues if politicians heard from enough of his people.

He pledged in 1950 to help mobilize blacks in Oklahoma. He never liked the word "militant." Instead Stewart wanted blacks in Oklahoma to get excited about their heritage and give their time and money to the fight for equality. Stewart wrote, "If this nation is to make itself secure as a democratic bastion and restore its moral influence abroad, it must proceed without delay to the eradication of Jim Crow from all phases of American life."[4]

Stewart called upon all Americans to remove the stigma of discrimination and segregation from national life. He contacted churches of all faiths, organized labor, fraternal organizations, civic associations, and any interested individual to build a coalition of civil rights fighters and activists. He raised money to continue the campaign for equality in every corner of Oklahoma.

Stewart's attitude toward the methods of achieving equality changed partly because of the indisputable fact that Jim Crow was alive and well in Oklahoma in 1950. As a recognized civil rights leader, Stewart was often the first to know about discrimination. When black visitors from Memphis were denied the right to play golf at the Lincoln Park Golf Course, they wrote to Stewart, "They were very insulting when we asked if we could play. We play in Chicago quite a lot and played in Kansas City, and Wichita last month. We called the other city courses, a Woodson course and the Hefner Lake course, and they hung up on us and made some remarks."[5]

Segregation was still present in Oklahoma in theaters, train, and bus stations, hotels, restaurants, and even in the State Capitol where signs on the lavatory doors read "White Gentlemen" and "White Ladies," a situation that resulted in a scathing editorial in *The Black Dispatch*:

> This is a picture of American segregation as it grovels in the very gutter of selfishness and marble-hearted inconsistency. Any system that would deny a human being the right to relieve his bowels and his bladder when nature demands is inhuman, cruel, and merciless. Race hate becomes ferocious and savage when it stoops to such depths. [6]

Dunjee encouraged Stewart's new attitude, reminding him that "Someone has said 'no one has any more rights than he will take,' and to beat the Jim Crow filth of segregation on railroad cars in Oklahoma will take a little courage, added to a court decision." [7]

When it appeared the Ku Klux Klan was being reorganized in Oklahoma County in the early 1950s, Stewart rallied his troops and organized a boycott of the newspaper in Jones, in northeast Oklahoma County, that had run an advertisement soliciting interest in the Klan. Stewart said, "There are 35,000 Negroes in northeast Oklahoma County and we don't intend to be pushed around. . . No yellow belly with a hood over his ugly face is going to run us out."[8]

Stewart was no stranger to City Council meetings in Oklahoma City. If the black community had a problem that needed to be brought to the attention of City leaders, Stewart asked to be placed on the agenda and spoke from his heart of the plight of his neighbors. (Courtesy *The Daily Oklahoman.*)

Stewart and Tulsa attorney Amos T. Hall represented Oklahoma in Washington, D.C. in January, 1950, in what was called the National Emergency Civil Rights Mobilization. More than 3,500 delegates representing 60 national organizations, including the NAACP, converged on the United States Capitol to demand passage of President Harry Truman's civil rights program.

Stewart and Hall called on Oklahoma United States Senators Robert S. Kerr and Elmer Thomas to solicit their help. Both Democratic senators were already on record as being in favor of Truman's civil rights package although Stewart was unhappy with Senator Kerr for being "evasive" about revealing his position on certain technical votes expected in the Senate, votes which could ultimately determine the success or failure of civil rights legislation.

Stewart also met with Congressman Mike Monroney. The two had become close friends with Monroney often asking Stewart for advice and counsel on equality issues. Monroney had won overwhelming support from the black community for his voting record on anti-poll tax legislation in 1949.

After the Washington meeting, Stewart and Roy Wilkins, acting secretary of the NAACP, drafted a check list for local branches of the organization to use in applying pressure on members of Congress. Branches were urged to educate the masses with literature distributions, public meetings, and letter-writing campaigns, and to mobilize other organizations and individuals.

Stewart rose through the ranks of the national structure of the NAACP. He was elected a regional director in 1948 and grew close to the national leadership, including Roy Wilkins who guided the NAACP during the apex of America's civil rights movement.

Stewart won membership awards for the Oklahoma City Branch with aggressive membership drives in the early 1950s. He recognized that white ministers of many different church denominations were sympathetic to the cause for equality. Stewart asked his board members to contact local ministers to see if they were interested in becoming members of the NAACP. Stewart followed up the contact with a letter that explained the connection between church groups and the NAACP:

Seventy-five percent of our local meetings are held in church buildings and better than 50 percent of our local presidents are ministers. We feel that our aims and program have a like direction or tendency with the program of God's church since our work is toward full citizenship and equal rights for all men. We seek to win first-class citizenship within the constitutional framework of our democracy and have not resorted to any other means.[9]

Stewart welcomed Duke Ellington to Oklahoma City on the Duke's 75th birthday. Stewart made Ellington an honorary member of the local YMCA and used the occasion to promote membership in the Y.

Jimmy Stewart, a
champion of
equality for all.

1951 was a banner year for the annual membership drive for the Oklahoma City Branch, thanks to Stewart's leadership and to the hard work of membership chairman Mrs. D. J. Diggs. In the annual report for 1951 Stewart urged members to become more active. He quoted the Bible, saying, "The Good Book says faith without works is dead. I'm tired of these drugstore and fireside quarterbacks talking about what the NAACP should do yet the majority won't or don't think enough of us to join or never find time to come to meetings. There are far too many Negroes in this town willing to slide back into hell and human slavery than to stand up and be counted."[10]

Stewart knew the value of delegation of responsibility in a large organization. He carefully appointed an executive committee and standing committees with duties involving everything from fundraising to selection of meeting places.

Stewart closed his 1951 report with a call for rededication, "It is my hope that we may, next year, rededicate ourselves to the cause of human rights, evermore keeping in mind the admonition of the prophet Zechariah who said 'Not by might, nor by power, but by my Spirit, said the Lord of Host.' " [11]

Oklahoma City's First Methodist Church invited Stewart to address its members at a Young People's Forum in October, 1951. In a rousing speech about parental responsibility and blame for the ills of children, Stewart applauded a nationwide "Back to the Church and Home" movement supported by the Church Department of the NAACP. Stewart said the program was "a sedative for ills of the day."[12]

Stewart leaned heavily on local churches for monetary support of the NAACP and for providing a meeting place for the organization. Meetings in 1951 were held at Quayle Methodist Church, Avery Chapel A.M.E. Church, Allen Chapel Church, Wall's Chapel Church, Tabernacle Baptist Church, Shiloh Baptist Church, Church of the Living God, Fairview Baptist Church, St. John Missionary Baptist Church, and Union Baptist Church.

In 1951 Stewart recruited a former white school teacher, Caroline E. M. Burks, to chair the local NAACP publicity committee.

It was stroke of genius. Miss Burks worked day and night to publicize the good works of the NAACP. She was assisted by Caroline Countee, D. J. Diggs, Carl Bode, Reverend J. C. West, Reverend W. K. Jackson, Meredith Mathews, Cernoria Johnson, Dr. Byron Biscoe, and Roscoe Dunjee on the publicity committee which was called by Roy Wilkins "the most active publicity committee anywhere in the world."

Miss Burks minced no words in telling the white community to change its attitude, "Negroes want their place in the sun, the good things of life, and first class citizenship. They ask that white persons bury their prejudices and identify themselves, through action, in securing full citizenship for Negroes."[13]

Miss Burks held two degrees from Columbia University and came to Oklahoma after she was told in Oregon, "We don't have laws against Negroes here. Why don't you go back to Oklahoma where they do?" Burks did, and made a difference in the Oklahoma civil rights struggle for the next 15 years.

Stewart often spent six nights a week in meetings of NAACP committees or other organizations of which he was a member. He actively participated in the Community Chest drive, the Negro Chamber of Commerce, and served as a member of the executive committee and as secretary of the Committee of Management of the Fourth Street YMCA. Stewart was much sought after as a master of ceremonies for many events around town. His dry humor left audiences waiting for punchlines.

Stewart was on the original Committee of Management for the YMCA when it began planning construction of a facility in the black community in 1946. The committee's membership included F. D. Moon, Roscoe Dunjee, W. J. Edwards, Dr. W. L. Haywood, Dr. J. M. Littlepage, A. D. Mathues, J. W. Sanford, Dr. W. H. Slaughter, and Reverend E. W. Perry. Stewart was chairman of the publicity committee that promoted the dedication of the YMCA's new building on Fourth Street in February, 1952.

NINE

A NATIONAL CONVENTION

STEWART DREAMED of holding the national convention of the NAACP in Oklahoma City. In early 1951 he developed a proposal to invite the national organization to meet in Oklahoma's capital city for its annual conclave in 1952.

At first national officials were less than excited about Oklahoma City hosting the convention. Roy Wilkins frankly expected the Time and Place Committee to select St. Louis, Missouri, or Cleveland, Ohio, because so many members of the NAACP were concentrated in the northeastern United States. Wilkins did not discourage Stewart from submitting a proposal but noted that Oklahoma City was "a little out of the way for heavy representation from all sections of the country."[1] Wilkins expected nearly 2,000 people for the convention in 1952 compared to the 300 delegates who attended the national convention of the NAACP in Oklahoma City in 1934.

Dunjee, who hosted the 1934 convention, privately urged Stewart to do everything in his power to land the 1952 convention. Dunjee used his influence as a member of the national NAACP Board of Directors to lobby members of the Time and Place Committee.

Stewart and a host of volunteers developed a comprehensive plan of action. To overcome national office fears of inadequate facilities, Stewart secured commitments from the Calvary Baptist Church, which seated more than 1,600 people, Taft Stadium, Page Stadium, and the Municipal Auditorium as sites for mass meetings expected at the convention.

Stewart and members of a special convention committee traveled to Atlanta in late 1951 to present their proposal to NAACP officials who were persuaded to select Oklahoma City as the official site of the 1952 national NAACP convention. The work had just begun.

Using his organizational ability, Stewart selected proven leaders in the black community to head major committees to support the national convention.

Meredith Mathews was named National Convention Coordinator as chairman of the Steering Committee. Mathews was Stewart's right-hand man to coordinate every activity of the convention. W. C. Price was chosen by Stewart as chairman of the Finance Committee. Price's primary function was to raise funds for

Hannah Atkins was the first black woman elected to the Oklahoma House of Representatives. She later served as Oklahoma Secretary of State.

convention expenses. Cernoria Johnson was chairman of the Registration Committee whose assignment was setting up an adequate system of registration of delegates to the convention.

Hannah Atkins was tabbed by Stewart to chair the Entertainment Committee, to be composed of not less than 50 people gathered from social clubs and fraternal organizations. The Entertainment Committee was in charge of planning banquets, benefit movies, dances, fashion shows and contests to raise money for the convention. It was a choice assignment for Atkins, who became a brilliant star among black leaders in Oklahoma. In 1968 she became the first black woman elected to the Oklahoma House of Representatives. President Jimmy Carter appointed Atkins as a United States delegate to the United Nations General Assembly. She served eight years as a member of the Democratic National Committee and three years as a commissioner of the United Nations Educational, Scientific and Cultural Organization (UNESCO). Governor Henry Bellmon chose her as Oklahoma Secretary of State in 1987, the highest state government post ever held by a black woman in Oklahoma.

Douglass High School Principal F. D. Moon was the chairman of the Radio and Television Committee whose job was to enlighten the public about the NAACP and the convention.

Mrs. H. A. Berry was chosen to head the Publicity and Public Relations Committee. Stewart asked Mrs. Berry to "Keep NAACP activities in the eyes of the public through all mediums possible."

Famed music teacher Zelia N. Breaux was named chairman of the Music Committee. This committee was asked to furnish all music for the national convention.

A. D. Matheus was chairman of the Welcome and Transportation Committee. The duties of that committee were to make visitors "as welcome and comfortable as possible as well as offer any assistance, directions, and courtesies possible." The committee also coordinated all transportation such as courtesy cars and buses for sightseeing tours.

Reverend William J. Harvey, III chaired the Program Committee, charged with finalizing all parts of each program of the convention ranging from who was going to sing the national anthem to who would pray over each session. The Youth Committee, asked to make the necessary arrangements to entertain, direct and assist youth delegates, was headed by Lucille McClendon. Ed Held and Roy Dawson co-chaired the Ushers Committee, whose members were to seat delegates and guests. Roscoe Dunjee was appointed by Stewart to chair the Souvenir Program Committee.

After months of planning and involvement on the part of hundreds of Oklahoma Cityans, the forty-third annual convention of the NAACP opened in Oklahoma City on June 24, 1952. The souvenir program touted Oklahoma City as "Out Where The West Begins." In his column in *The Black Dispatch* the week before the convention, Stewart told his readers he was "beat to the gills" by all the preparation.

Stewart, as president of the host NAACP chapter, presided over the opening meeting of the convention on Tuesday night, June 24 at Calvary Baptist Church. Stewart welcomed the nearly 2,000 delegates to Oklahoma City.

After a musical program by the Twilight Time Chorale, directed by Tracy Sylvester, and welcomed by Oklahoma City Mayor Allen Street and Calvary Baptist Pastor Reverend William J. Harvey, III, NAACP administrator Roy Wilkins made the keynote address.

Wilkins blasted race bias in America, calling segregation the "root of the race problem." The NAACP said the world was asking embarrassing questions about America, about a country that would leave children to be cheated in ramshackle segregated schools.

Wilkins promised that the civil rights fight would not be lost:

The hate bombs of this year will fail. They will fail because we
will cry out, and not cower in silence. They will fail because we
are Americans who are determined to have nothing less than
the American heritage. They will fail because long years of
lynching only make us more angry, more determined, and more
active. This desperate revival of violence will fail. [2]

Wilkins was critical of federal and state government reactions to destructive riots in Cicero, Illinois, the previous summer. He pledged to the cheering crowd, "Without fear we march forward. Our meeting in Oklahoma City is an unmistakable expression of our unity of thought and action."[3]

On Wednesday NAACP official Walter White and other dignitaries led workshops. The Wednesday night mass meeting was addressed by Dr. Louis T. Wright of New York City, the chairman of the national board of the NAACP.

Attorney Thurgood Marshall led a panel discussion during the business session on Thursday morning. The topic was racial segregation and how it affected the nation, the community, and America's children. Members of the panel were Professor Kenneth Clark of the City College of New York, Professor Kenneth J. Morland of William and Mary College, *Journal of Negro Education* editor Charles H. Thompson, and Robert C. Weaver, chairman of the National Committee Against Discrimination in Housing.

On Thursday afternoon Marshall led a vigorous discussion of plans for the NAACP to continue the fight against segregation in the courts of the land, from municipal courts to the United States Supreme Court.

During the convention more than 400 delegates attended a testimonial dinner in the Zebra Room of the Civic Center for Roscoe Dunjee. F. D. Moon, and Walter White lauded the editor for his unselfish years of devotion to the cause of freedom.

Stewart hardly slept during the five days of the convention. He had somehow rallied more than 800 volunteers to man the hundreds of assignments necessary to orchestrate a successful convention. Stewart was ably assisted by the Oklahoma Association of Negro Teachers, and its president H. F. V. Wilson; the Oklahoma State Federation of Colored Women, headed by Ellen Marguerite Roberson; and dozens of other civic, social, and fraternal organizations in the black community.

The June, 1952, convention was just months before the presidential election which pitted Republican Dwight D. Eisenhower against Democrat Adlai Stevenson. NAACP by-laws forbade the

Welcome NAACP Delegates . . . .

James E. Stewart, local president of the National Association for the Advancement of Colored People, takes this opportunity to welcome you delegates to Oklahoma City on behalf of the Oklahoma Natural Gas Company.

Stewart, who served for three years with the Marines during World War II, has been a member of Oklahoma Natural's organization for the past 15 years and at the present time is manager of the Company's East Fourth street office.

Oklahoma Natural joins him in wishing for you a most successful convention and hopes that your stay in Oklahoma City will be a pleasant one.

OKLAHOMA NATURAL
Gas Company

Oklahoma Natural Gas Company's advertisement for the official program of the 1952 national NAACP convention held in Oklahoma City. (Courtesy Oklahoma Natural Gas Company.)

endorsement of any candidate or political party. However, it was no secret that most black leaders, including Stewart and the local branch of the NAACP, supported the civil rights plank of the proposed Democratic platform. A resolution was passed recognizing that the NAACP "has an inescapable political responsibility and obligation to our country and to that segment of the population of our country to whose advancement this organization is dedicated."[4]

Other resolutions called segregation "still the evil root from which stem all the sinister manifestations of bigotry, of intolerance, of racism, of cynical defeatism."

The NAACP delegates, 750 official delegates from 37 states, acknowledged the major victories scored by the organization and its legal team headed by Thurgood Marshall. The right to vote, the right to equality in education, the right to freedom of residence, the right to a fair trial, and the right to unsegregated service in the armed forces were listed as achievements.

However, one resolution read, "Despite these victories the evil roots of segregation remain in many parts of the country, reaching down deep and contaminating the subsoil of American culture." The NAACP delegates accepted the challenge. In the Preamble to the resolutions passed at the convention, delegates stated:

> The responsibility to annihilate this pernicious evil is not only that of the Negro but of the entire nation. Here in Oklahoma City at the mid-point in the second year of the last half of the 20th century we again rededicate ourselves to this task; and mob violence, cowardly bombings; intimidations, whether by hooded or un-hooded groups, will not cause us to turn back. . . With redoubled energy we shall renew, increase and intensify the attack through legal actions, through sponsorship of legislative measures and through enlightened public opinion.[5]

Delegates approved a resolution calling upon officials at all levels of government to stop police brutality against blacks, "Unrestrained police brutality is a contagion which spreads from one minority to another until it ultimately causes a breakdown of law enforcement in the entire community."

A nine-point program outlining the NAACP's stand on civil rights legislation was adopted. Segregation solely because of race or color was labeled "offensive." Members pledged to work for the enactment of federal legislation prohibiting discrimination in employment and housing and making lynching and other mob assaults a federal crime.

On the final day of the convention United States Senator Hubert Humphrey of Minnesota spoke to delegates via telephone hookup from Washington, D. C., Humphrey, an advocate of federal action outlawing segregation rather than leaving it up to the states said, "States-rightsers are states-wrongers."

Walter White turned to presidential politics in a final address to the convention. He said he was shocked at General Dwight D. Eisenhower's views on civil rights. White warned Democrats not to choose a Southerner who might be weak on civil rights, "If Democrats want to commit political hara-kiri let them nominate

Richard Russell [United States Senator from Georgia], Robert Kerr [United States Senator from Oklahoma] or any other anti-civil rights candidate for either place on the ticket. If the Democrats nominate anyone whose record is bad on civil rights, they can kiss the Negro vote good-bye."[7]

During the Sunday session Roy Wilkins wanted to honor Stewart. He told the gathering, "I want Stewart, who has had the major responsibility for our delightful stay to come up and take a bow." Unfortunately, Stewart was home taking a well-deserved nap and missed the accolade.

When the convention ended on June 29, Stewart and Dunjee drove Thurgood Marshall and Wilkins to the airport. Both national leaders had nothing but high praise for the efforts of Stewart and his army of volunteers in hosting what Marshall called "the best meeting we have ever had."[8]

TEN
LOCAL AND STATE ISSUES

STEWART was always the first in line to volunteer for any assignment to further the fight for civil rights. He frequently paid his own expenses to national meetings and trips to Washington, D.C., to visit with Oklahoma's congressional delegation. The national officers of the NAACP knew they could call upon Stewart anytime to speak on college campuses or hold organizational workshops for new local branches. However, Stewart's heart and spirit were in Oklahoma and his passion burned brightest for equality for his neighbors in the Sooner State.

Stewart's role as a leader in the civil rights struggle was often painful for his family. The Stewart children were frightened on Christmas night in 1951 when they awoke to see a cross burning on the front lawn. The cowardly perpetrators were never identified.

Stewart threw himself wholeheartedly into representing the views of blacks at any meeting of any organization, black or white. He was often away from home five or six evenings each week. Daughter Zandra later reflected that, in a sense, her father belonged to the whole community.

Stewart did not spend as much time with his children as he would have desired. He tried to make up for the loss of quality time by planning interesting vacations and by conducting what he called "learning" sessions. Stewart frequently took his children aside and talked seriously about the importance of being honest, hard-working, and a man, or woman, of their word. One of the few times Stewart was ever truly disappointed in anyone was when he had been lied to by a friend or co-worker.

Mae Lois was in charge of the majority of the discipline Jimmy, Jr. and Zandra received. When Mae Lois was at her wit's end as Stewart arrived home from work or from a meeting, Mae Lois might yell, "Jimmy, whip these kids."

In 1950 Oklahoma City Chamber of Commerce officials asked the Negro Chamber of Commerce to support a citywide bond issue to finance capital improvements, including the construction of six new fire stations. It was Stewart who asked pointed questions at a meeting to consider the bond issue. Stewart reminded fellow Negro Chamber of Commerce members that for years city officials had refused to hire blacks as firefighters. The city's perennial excuse was that no job openings existed. Stewart told the audience that it was unreasonable to expect whites to be fired so blacks could be hired, but with six new fire stations, surely blacks could be hired. After Stewart's quiet, but impassioned speech, the Negro Chamber of Commerce delayed a decision until Stewart could meet with the mayor and members of the city council.

Backers of the bond issue were alarmed and requested a meeting with black leaders. No progress was reported from the first meeting. At a second meeting, white leaders said they had no legal authority to make any promise regarding the hiring of blacks. Stewart's pert response was, "Then we don't have the legal authority to tell you that black people will support the bond issue."

A third meeting brought a promise from the city council and mayor that blacks would be hired by the fire department if the black community supported the bond issue. There was a handshake followed by a bold headline in the next morning's issue of *The Daily Oklahoman*, "Stewart Okays Bond Issue."

The city was true to its promise. A dozen black men, Cecil Dixon, E. K. Russell, Herb Ford, Algie Lawrence, M. O. Nelson, M. A. Franklin, Willard Jenkins, Carl Holmes, Bob Summers, Charles Wright, J. B. Coffey, and J. H. Young, were hired and assigned to Station Number Nine on Northeast Ninth Street. All but two of the men remained until retirement. Holmes advanced to the position of Administrative Chief of the Oklahoma City Fire Department. A plaque honoring "The Original 12" hangs in the Oklahoma Firefighters' Museum.

Stewart was not afraid to ask white leaders for jobs for blacks in exchange for his support of politicians or political issues. When he was invited to help oust the county attorney in Oklahoma County, Stewart asked for, and received, a commitment from candidate James W. "Bill" Berry to hire a black assistant county attorney. When Berry won, Stewart and Dr. Byron Biscoe recommended senior University of Oklahoma law student John E. Green for the job. When Green graduated and passed the bar examination, he became the state's first black prosecutor, and served Oklahoma well for decades as a state and federal prosecutor.

Stewart never was too busy to help others. His children remember him being detained at the grocery store by some woman whose son needed a job. Stewart always stopped and pulled his pencil and pad from his pocket and took down important information.

Stewart placed hundreds of black teenagers in jobs in government and the private sector. However, he would not ask anyone to give jobs to his own children. He never wanted to be accused of leading the civil rights struggle for personal gain. His refusal to help his own children land "cushy" summer jobs was a bone of contention between Stewart and Mae Lois, one of the few bumpy spots in an otherwise incredibly smooth marriage. Jimmy, Jr. remembers his mother confronting his father with the fact that he had placed neighbor children in jobs in air-conditioned buildings downtown while his own children earned peanuts as lifeguards at the local YMCA pool.

Stewart's telephone regularly rang into the late-night hours. Many people wanted to help in the struggle for equality. Some wanted to criticize Stewart's leadership. Still others had legitimate complaints of injustice that needed to be addressed by NAACP leaders.

In 1952 Maryland State College Athletic Director V. E. McCain, a black man who once coached at Douglass High School, was refused service at the lunch counter at Will Rogers World Airport. When a well-dressed bystander, University of Indiana President H. B. Wells intervened, the manager of the SkyChief Restaurant again refused to allow McCain to sit with whites at the counter, offering instead to "prepare a place in the back of the restaurant."

McCain complained to American Airlines, "The incident involved considerable embarrassment for me, plus physical discomfort, since there was no place for me to secure a meal in comfortable circumstances."[1] President Wells asked a black porter who the local head of the NAACP was. Fortunately, the man knew Stewart and gave Wells his telephone number.

Stewart entered the fray and contacted American Airlines, the carrier on which McCain and Wells were booked for a flight to Washington, D.C. Within hours the complaint reached the very top of American Airlines, to the office of president C. R. Smith in New York City.

Stewart, armed with letters and information from McCain and Wells, expressed his displeasure in a telephone call with Smith. Within days American Airlines announced a new policy prohibiting segregation by restaurant lessees.

In 1953 Stewart joined forces with United States Senator Mike Monroney to place blacks in the better-paying positions at the Federal Aviation Administration facility at Will Rogers World Airport. Blacks only had served as janitors until Stewart convinced Monroney to take an active part in demanding blacks be given equal opportunities for jobs at the center which later would be named for Monroney.

Stewart strongly believed in recognizing publicly the achievements of citizens in the community. In 1953 he spearheaded a testimonial banquet for Oklahoma City police detective Ernest E. Jones who was promoted to lieutenant after 26 years on the force. Jones was one of the first black officers hired by the Oklahoma City Police Department.

Stewart even recruited Thurgood Marshall to help honor Jones. Stewart wrote Marshall, "Now I doubt if a poor New York lawyer has any cash to drop in the till, we plan to give Jones a swell gift, however we do want you to write a testimonial of about 40 words to appear on the program."[2]

Jones, according to Stewart, was "a regular Joe, a natural police officer who has never been an Uncle Tom in the performance of his duty."[3]

Stewart had two reasons for the Jones celebration. He wanted to honor Jones and salute city officials for promoting a black man to lieutenant on the police force, a rarity in the South in 1953.

Roscoe Dunjee was Stewart's mentor and hero. However, the two champions of civil rights did not always see eye-to-eye on every issue. At the close of the 1952 NAACP national convention in Oklahoma City, Dunjee criticized the NAACP for not moving quicker in the civil rights struggle. The criticism came even though Dunjee was a member of the national NAACP Board of Directors.

Dunjee found fault in NAACP leaders for not having more members in the black community. Dunjee editorialized, "Do not permit the fanfare and shouting during convention to mislead you. The NAACP is important but only has 200,000 members of the 15 million Negroes in America."[4] The editor wrote that passive resistance would not work, that it was wrong for only 200,000 blacks to be involved while the rest "are looking upward for manna from heaven."[5]

In classic Dunjeeism, *The Black Dispatch* editorial page spewed forth, "Why should we storm about murders and riots and at the same time expect justice, liberty, and freedom to fall from the skies without any effort whatsoever on the part of the American black man. We are still spiritually enslaved despite Lincoln's freedom and the NAACP." [6]

Dunjee's specific complaint with Stewart was the failure of the NAACP to bring V. E. McCain back to Oklahoma City and support a lawsuit against the SkyChief Restaurant at Will Rogers World Airport.

Stewart responded to Dunjee's criticism with a nine-page letter detailing the victories won by the local branch of the NAACP. Stewart explained that using McCain, who lived in Maryland, as a plaintiff in a civil rights case was impractical and would result in unnecessary expenses. Stewart assured Dunjee that the incident at the airport would not go unchallenged, "The Oklahoma City Branch will carry thru in like manner at the airport restaurant the same as at Lincoln Park and the Municipal Auditorium but we can't under God's Heaven act without a cause or a case."[7]

Stewart also used the occasion to applaud the efforts of NAACP members, "While some people are out making the rounds of the taverns or playing bridge, let's think of the faithful NAACP workers who are ringing doorbells in the process of securing more followers of the cause. . . They are unsung heroes." Stewart asked Dunjee to "be more tolerant as ye would have others be."[8]

In the summer of 1953 Stewart called upon NAACP Regional Legal Counsel U. Simpson Tate to assist the Oklahoma City Branch to end segregation at Lincoln Park and the Municipal Auditorium in Oklahoma City.

Officially the Park Board allowed blacks to visit the park only on Thursdays. However, after Stewart, accompanied by Tate and other lawyers, conferred with city officials and explained the latest United States Supreme Court rulings, the Park Board backed down.

Publicly, the board announced it would study the issue. However, Stewart sent out press releases to local newspapers and radio stations indicating that blacks were free to use Lincoln Park seven days a week. Stewart was so bold as to promise to make the bond, pay the fine, court costs, and attorney's fees if any black was arrested at Lincoln Park. Stewart threatened to file a lawsuit for false arrest against any police officer who arrested a black at the park solely because of his or her race. The threat was enough. Lincoln Park was desegregated peacefully.[9]

One issue close to Stewart's heart was housing. As a poverty-stricken child himself, he knew the suffering caused by inadequate housing. In 1953 blacks were among the most poorly housed Americans, often crowded into the least desirable sections of town, in less than habitable dwellings.

Stewart spoke at the opening of the new Garden Oaks Addition in northeast Oklahoma City in March, 1953. Adequate housing was on his mind. He pointed out that recent statistics from the National Housing Agency showed 17 percent of blacks in Oklahoma City lived in substandard housing, while only 10 percent of whites were in the same predicament.

As whites moved toward the outskirts of the original limits of Oklahoma City, blacks expanded into neighborhoods vacated by the whites and occupied the decaying houses. Stewart was concerned that even black families of moderate or substantial means had no incentive to invest in old and dilapidated houses.

Stewart called upon government to clear slums, redevelop salvageable houses, and build public housing to supplement private construction. He warned, "Unless far more imagination and energy are devoted to the problem, the situation may within the lifetime of many of you within the sound of my voice become appalling beyond belief."10

Stewart urged the private sector to recognize that blacks were a ready market for new housing. He challenged the audience, "So long as large numbers of our brothers are wretchedly housed, we can ill-afford to shelve the problem. . . The cost, in terms of national unity and productivity, is too great to turn our heads."11

In early 1953, the Oklahoma Planning and Resources Board, the state agency charged with operating the state park system, announced plans to build a segregated area for use by blacks in the Sequoyah State Park.

Stewart, Dunjee, State NAACP President Dr. H. W. Williamston, and NAACP lawyers met with the Planning and Resources Board to protest the plan. At first, it appeared park officials listened and would disband their plans. However, after state newspapers announced that the segregated park area would be built, Stewart worked with regional NAACP lawyers and Ada Lois Sipuel Fisher to draft a lawsuit. They chose as plaintiff Jake Simmons, Jr. of Muskogee.

Simmons was the perfect plaintiff for the lawsuit. He was highly respected and recognized as the most successful black oil entrepreneur in America. He later served as state president of the NAACP in Oklahoma. Supreme Court Justice Hardy Summers, who was Simmons' personal lawyer before taking the bench, said Simmons was successful as a civil rights leader because of his absolute devotion to non-violent methods of protest. Simmons was adamant in his advice to blacks to never retaliate for wrongs inflicted.[12] Simmons and Stewart worked closely on Oklahoma civil rights issues, joined at the hip by their often unpopular belief that non-violent protest and negotiation would, in the end, be the only means by which blacks could attain equal treatment and respect.[13]

The lawsuit against the Planning and Resources Board alleged that any attempt to segregate the races in state parks was repugnant to the United States Constitution. After being challenged by the lawsuit, the board passed a new resolution which still called for the construction of the area at Sequoyah State Park but deleted any mention of declaring its use only for blacks. The new resolution also committed the state to follow the laws of the land.

Because there was no longer a controversy, the Oklahoma Supreme Court dismissed the case. Stewart believed the lawsuit was necessary to make the point that Oklahoma blacks would not stand for segregation, especially since the United States Supreme Court was quickly wiping away all legal justification for separation of the races in public facilities.

Stewart was upset in July, 1953, when newly-elected President Eisenhower nominated South Carolina Governor James F. Byrnes as the United States delegate to the General Assembly of the United Nations. Byrnes had a long record of opposing equality for blacks. He openly threatened to abolish the South Carolina public school system if segregation was ever outlawed by the United States Supreme Court.

Stewart wired President Eisenhower, "By proven words and actions, Governor Byrnes is unfit to represent our American way of life." To United States Senators Robert S. Kerr and Mike Monroney Stewart's telegram was straight and to the point, "For God's sake stop the confirmation of Governor Byrnes. He has openly and savagely opposed equal rights and our organization strongly feels that he should not be put in a position to give aid and comfort to the forces of bigotry and hate."[14]

Over widespread objections from labor unions, civil rights organizations, and Senator Monroney, the Senate confirmed Byrnes's nomination.

As college classes began in September, 1954, some Oklahoma institutions of higher learning continued to refuse to admit blacks. The NAACP filed suit against Eastern Oklahoma A&M College at Wilburton and on behalf of a young black man, Ulysses Grant, who had attempted to enroll at El Reno Junior College. Both cases were successfully completed in time for the students to enroll at mid-term.

In late 1954 Stewart convinced U. Simpson Tate and the regional office of the NAACP to file suit against the Oklahoma College for Women in Chickasha to allow black students to enroll. Clydia E. Troullier was a mother of two who was denied admission solely because of her color. However, before the case could be heard by a three-judge federal panel, the college voluntarily allowed blacks to enroll. After several church-affiliated colleges responded in like fashion, Stewart declared that "the entire college system of Oklahoma is open to all."

A headline on an editorial in *The Daily Oklahoman* in January, 1955, offended Stewart, most blacks, and many whites in Oklahoma. The editorial criticized Governor Raymond Gary's choice of automobile dealer Mead Norton as chairman of the Oklahoma Turnpike Authority. The editorial headline read, "A Nigger in the Woodpile."

Stewart called the newspaper and was told by Carl Stuart that he saw nothing wrong with the caption. Stewart sent a telegram to Governor Gary, "Oklahoma Negroes deeply resent the ugly connotation. . . White and black people have reached a higher level in brotherhood than is indicated by this vicious throwback to the days I had hoped had gone forever."[15]

Stewart polled members of the local NAACP branch executive committee who agreed that pickets should be placed outside the offices of the newspaper at Fourth and Broadway in downtown

Oklahoma City. Within hours, a dozen pickets with signs denouncing the newspaper's use of the word "nigger" were in place.

The pickets were removed only after newspaper publisher E. K. Gaylord issued an apology. Gaylord called the use of the racial term an "unfortunate selection, was hastily used and we are sorry." Gaylord said his paper meant no offense and pledged to continue to support bi-racial harmony in the community.[16]

ELEVEN
SCHOOL DESEGREGATION

ALL FORMS OF SEGREGATION were sickening to Stewart, but the segregation of public schools was the most onerous. Stewart recognized the importance of education for any child to be successful in life. He was appalled that black children did not have the same opportunities for education as white children. From Stewart's earliest years as a civil rights activist, he pledged to fight for integration of public schools for as long as it took to achieve the goal.

Years of uncertainty and conflict over the legality of separate schools for black children came to a head in the United States Supreme Court in the early 1950s. The high court accepted jurisdiction of five cases brought on behalf of black children who were denied admission to all-white schools. The cases came from South Carolina, Kansas, Virginia, Delaware, and the District of Columbia.

The Supreme Court chose the Kansas case, *Brown v. Board of Education of Topeka, Kansas,* to make what may have been the most significant decision in American jurisprudence. On May 17, 1954, the Court unanimously concluded that separate education facilities were inherently unequal.

The decision clearly outlawed separate schools even if the physical facilities were equal. The court reasoned that education was the most important function of state and local government, was the foundation of good citizenship, and that equal education opportunities were mandated by the constitution. The momentous decision concluded, "To separate them from others of similar age and qualifications solely because of their race generates a feeling of inferiority as to their status in the community that may affect their hearts and minds in a way unlikely ever to be undone."[1]

Even though *Brown* was a Kansas case, the ruling directly affected schools in Oklahoma and 16 other states where segregation was mandated or allowed by state law.

Brown sent a shock wave throughout American education, especially in the South. Newspapers throughout the world heralded the end of segregation in education. At the United Nations the decision was regarded as a great step in improving America's image in third-world countries.

Stewart never forgot the call he received from NAACP attorney Thurgood Marshall on the afternoon that the Supreme Court publicly announced its decision in the *Brown* case. Stewart and Marshall had talked about the possibility of such a decision for years. The NAACP had never given up in the struggle to dismantle desegregation. Marshall simply told Stewart, "It's finally over. We won." Marshall's only disappointment was that the Court had not set a specific date for the end to segregation.[2]

Stewart sat in the quietness of his office and reflected on the years of visiting black schools with pitiful facilities and underpaid teachers. He closed his eyes and saw the faces of the black boys and girls who he believed were robbed of an equal education. Was it really over?

Stewart met with editor Dunjee and NAACP board members to draft a statement in response to the Supreme Court decision. Stewart's prepared statement read:

The Supreme Court decision not only made possible the freedom of the segregated, but also released the segregationist in a variety of ways. In the long run it is to the advantage of all, even in Oklahoma City at Classen and Central; Northeast and Harding, to implement the decision and to make the transition from segregation to integration as effectively and speedily as possible, for the freedom of none is safe so long as the freedom of one is in jeopardy.[3]

Stewart told the press that American education had been given a second chance to "come into its birthright, to conserve and transmit our heritage, and to give rise to the full stature of its potential."[4]

Editor Dunjee wrote in *The Black Dispatch*, "The Monday ruling cements all Americans together. There will perhaps be a great amount of implementation involved before authorities in all of the states will get around to this line of thinking, but this is our individual belief as we survey the passing of *Plessy v. Ferguson*."[5]

Oklahoma Governor Johnston Murray, and his successor, Raymond Gary, showed statesmanlike leadership in cautioning against overreaction to the *Brown* decision. Both men pledged to abide by the law as stated by the Supreme Court. The state legislature scrapped the old system of separate tax levies for black schools and submitted to the people a constitutional amendment revamping school finance laws. When opponents cried that passage of State Question 368 would spell the end to segregated education, Governor Gary strongly urged voters to approve the question. Voters listened and overwhelmingly passed the amendment by a vote of 231,097 to 73,021 on April 5, 1955.

In her autobiography, Ada Lois Sipuel Fisher, herself a plaintiff in a landmark equality in education case, capsulated the effect of the Supreme Court's decision, "Admitting that separate education was inherently and inescapably unequal education, the Court finally placed a constitutional noose around Jim Crow's neck. The next year it sprang the gallows trap, holding in *Brown II* [a subsequent May, 1955, decision] that the South must dismantle its dual school system 'with all deliberate speed.' "[7]

It was a new day in Oklahoma. There was little violence that accompanied the social change of integration in the state. However there were problems.

Historian Jimmie Lewis Franklin wrote:

Both blacks and whites found themselves involved in a process which was totally new and which had been illegal for a half a century! If some discomfort and suspicion characterized the behavior of both groups, history could serve as a good explanation. Fundamental problems plagued blacks, such as the dismissal of teachers and the development of a spirit of cooperation among those with whom they did work. Some blacks also found that formerly all-black schools had been important cultural centers for them, but were now less so under integration.[8]

The law had demanded an end to segregation but there was still much to be done in Oklahoma to implement the mandated change. Stewart gathered state and local NAACP officials together in the fall of 1954 to develop a strategy for the peaceful transition to integrated schools.

Stewart was well known to Oklahoma school officials. In 1952, upon the advice of Thurgood Marshall, Stewart had presented a petition to the Oklahoma City Board of Education demanding the end of segregation. The petition, of course, went unheeded until the Supreme Court spoke in 1954.

After the *Brown* decision, Stewart and the local NAACP presented more petitions to the Oklahoma City Board of Education. The petitions reminded the school board of the new law of the land which required "good faith compliance at the earliest practicable date," and called upon the board to take immediate steps to reorganize the public schools "so that the children of public school age attending and entitled to attend public schools cannot be denied admission to any school or be required to attend any school solely because of race and color."[9]

The petitions charged the school board "to take immediate concrete steps leading to early elimination of segregation in the public schools. Please rest assured of our willingness to serve in any way we can to aid you in dealing with this question."[10]

The *Brown* desegregation decision had a domino effect upon other forms of segregation in Oklahoma. Stewart believed that the Supreme Court's opinion about separate facilities being inherently unequal facilities should also apply to other tax-supported institutions such as parks and auditoriums.

Shortly after the *Brown* decision, Stewart and NAACP regional counsel U. Simpson Tate met with Oklahoma City City Manager William Gill. Also at the meeting were Cernoria Johnson, executive director of the Oklahoma City Urban League; Douglass Principal F. D. Moon; and E. R. Reno, executive secretary of the Oklahoma City Council of Churches.

Stewart quietly threatened legal action against the city if blacks were prevented from using any public facility. The quiet threat was heeded by city officials. Without fanfare, all parks, auditoriums, swimming pools and other facilities in Oklahoma City were integrated immediately.

Stewart was angry with another leading black organization in Oklahoma City in 1954. The Urban League asked Oklahoma City Mayor Allen Street to appoint a 25-member human relations commission to focus on the peaceful transition to integrated schools. For some reason the league did not ask the NAACP to send an official representative. Stewart was livid, charging Cernoria Johnson, the executive secretary of the Urban League's Oklahoma City chapter, with being willing to present NAACP ideas to the human relations commission but unwilling to have the NAACP officially represented on the commission because of the fear of offending "some of their well-meaning friends."

Stewart believed the Urban League was not as active in the civil rights struggle as his organization and said the NAACP would not accept the "weak-kneed approach of the Urban League on the question of desegregating our public schools."[11] Stewart was saddened by the controversy because the president of the local chapter of the Urban League was none other than F. D. Moon, Stewart's compatriot on dozens of civil rights struggles over the last two decades.

Stewart proposed that the Oklahoma City NAACP branch refuse to support any group working for the desegregation of Oklahoma City schools unless it was represented on the governing board of the group. The February, 1955, meeting to discuss the proposed resolution was so heated that Stewart referred the matter to the NAACP branch executive committee. He wrote NAACP national administrator Roy Wilkins to ask advice on how to handle the situation and Wilkins responded by suggesting that no resolution attacking the Urban League be passed by the NAACP branch. "While the Urban League may be grabbing the newspaper headlines and commenting favorable upon the appointment of this commission as the realization of a dream of that organization and others in the community, our past experience with mayor's committees in Detroit [Michigan], and elsewhere has often been unsatisfactory. These bodies tend to represent a wide variety of viewpoints, mostly conservative. They exist upon the sufferance of the mayor and have little other than advisory powers."[12]

Part of Stewart's motivation for challenging the role of the Urban League was the advice of editor Dunjee who warned Stewart that the Urban League was too conservative. Dunjee feared that the entire desegregation process would be slowed if the Urban League, rather than the NAACP, became the apparent representative voice of the black community.

Dunjee supported Stewart in an editorial in *The Black Dispatch*, "We feel Mr. Stewart's position is valid and that the organization which brought about this change in the South should be recognized in any group having to do with race relations. Everyone knows but for the continued fight of the NAACP we would still have separate schools and there would in actuality be nothing to discuss respecting integration. No organization that has given as much time and thought to the question of civil rights as the NAACP should be entirely ignored if an honest effort is made to improve race relations."[13]

T. H. McDowell, the regional director of the National Conference of Christians and Jews, tried to intervene in the dispute between the NAACP and the Urban League. McDowell was perplexed with the dissension within the black community at a time when all organizations needed to work together, "It is a strange and tragic fact that many organizations dedicated to building better human and community relations, do not practice good human relations among themselves. Possibly this is because we are all human and carry vestiges of our carnal nature, *Galatians* 5:19-23—

note especially the social sins of strife, jealously, anger, selfishness, dissension, party spirit, envy and their concomitant virtues."[14]

After a few meetings between Stewart, Moon, and Mrs. Johnson, ruffled feathers were smoothed. The Urban League and the NAACP again joined hands in the fight to totally integrate Oklahoma City schools and society. The Human Relations Commission membership included Chamber of Commerce Manager Stanley Draper, United States Circuit Judge Alfred P. Murrah, Reverend W. K. Jackson, retired New York Yankee pitcher Allie Reynolds, Rabbi Israel Chodos, and Dr. W. McFerrin Stowe, pastor of St. Luke's Methodist Church, who served as temporary chairman of the group and invited Stewart to personally attend all meetings.

At the middle of the twentieth century, Oklahoma's black population was approximately 145,000. The black population became increasingly urban with large black communities in Oklahoma City and Tulsa. Therefore the spotlight on integration of public schools was on the state's two largest cities.

The Supreme Court heard additional arguments on school desegregation, and how quickly it should be accomplished, in early 1955. Stewart flew to Washington to attend the oral arguments before the high court. His dream of watching Thurgood Marshall in action faded as he stood in a line "as long as a drunk sailor's dream"[15] outside the Supreme Court building. Stewart called United States Senator Mike Monroney who came to Stewart's aid. In his newspaper column, Stewart reported on Monroney's help, "Within five minutes he was in the Marshall's office and within six minutes Your Man Friday was laying his big brown eyes on the highest court of our land for the first time."[16]

Stewart described the Supreme Court for his readers, "The building probably cost more than our state capitol and is far more beautiful. The courtroom is a massive place which seats close to 500 people."[17]

In June, 1955, Stewart and Dunjee met with State Superintendent of Schools Oliver Hodge to discuss implementation of the Supreme Court's mandate to integrate public schools. Hodge and

Governor Gary recommended that all school districts move as quickly as possible to end segregation. The Governor warned that districts would not receive state aid if they defied federal law.

Gary hailed from southern Oklahoma, Little Dixie, and shocked some supporters when he publicly said that prejudice and segregation were contrary to the will of God and should be ended. The governor refused to attend meetings in hotels or resorts that refused admission to blacks or other minorities.

Also in June, Stewart was called to Atlanta to an emergency conference of key NAACP leaders in the South. It was a historic meeting led by Roy Wilkins and Thurgood Marshall. Each of the southern states, including Oklahoma, reported on the progress of desegregation and promised quick and certain legal action should a school district fail to show good faith in the early elimination of segregation.

On the return trip to Oklahoma City, Stewart's airplane encountered turbulent weather. He wrote in "Jimmy Says," "The trip out of New Orleans [Louisiana] to Dallas [Texas] was the roughest going Your Man Friday has ever experienced on train, car or plane. The sign flashed up front to fasten our safety belts and the stewardess said we were about to run into some bad weather. Within two minutes we hit it and General Grant couldn't have frightened those rebels in Georgia more than the first time the plane dropped. Brother, I've long heard of that old hymn 'I Want to See Jesus' but this trip convinced me there's very little reason while 7,000 feet on the way up to see Him to have to drop all the way back to the ground and make a fresh start."[18]

Back in Oklahoma City Stewart insisted that the board of education integrate schools immediately. Tulsa school officials had already announced plans to fully integrate its schools at the opening of the 1955 school year. Stewart said, "There is no need of the capital city dragging its feet on this subject while Tulsa takes the lead."[19]

In early August, the board of education unveiled its plan for desegregation by re-drawing boundary lines for 13 of the school district's 77 elementary schools. Nine formerly black elementary schools and six traditionally white schools were designed to serve a mixed student population. However, nothing was proposed to facilitate integration of the high schools.[20]

Before classes began, officials at Central High School, an all-white school, would not allow a dozen black students to enroll, instead suggesting the students go back and talk to their parents about staying at Douglass High School. Stewart was furious and called for a meeting of parents and interested citizens at the Bethlehem Star Baptist Church.

Stewart held public meetings at various churches in northeast Oklahoma City in the two weeks before classes were scheduled to begin. Bulletins were distributed to homes, announcing that the desegregation policy of the school board would be discussed. They encouraged parents to enroll their high school students in the school "nearest to their residence."

The legal barrier to integration had been stricken to the ground by the highest court in the land. However, actual desegregation of Oklahoma City's classrooms would take awhile longer.

TWELVE

THE ATLANTA
MEETING

IN 1956 Stewart's solid leadership as president of the Oklahoma City Branch of the NAACP and as vice president of the state NAACP conference was rewarded with his elevation to an at-large position on the national board of the NAACP, the nation's largest civil rights organization.

Stewart brought vast experience to his new position. His tenacity and hard-work ethic was widely known among leaders of the NAACP. Stewart had served on the Region Six NAACP board since 1946. In 11 years he never missed a regional board meeting. For much of that time Stewart shouldered the responsibility of raising funds from local and state branches to finance the operation of the regional office. Region Six was recognized as the most influential and active region within the NAACP until disputes over methods of accomplishing civil rights split regional leaders in 1954.

It was no secret that Stewart was part of the "majority caucus" of the national NAACP Board of Directors. He was a strong supporter of Executive Director Roy Wilkins. Stewart vociferously opposed attempts of more liberal elements to take over the NAACP. He worked hard against what he called "alien and devisive forces" that proposed unlawful and violent means to achieve racial desegregation.

Stewart was proud of his efforts to keep any talk of communistic ideas out of the NAACP national leadership. He believed his work allowed the NAACP to remain the "strongest, most respected, most feared and yet the most effective civil rights organization in the world."[1]

1956 was a benchmark year in the civil rights struggle in the United States. Public schools were desegregating at a euphoric pace despite the "Southern Manifesto," signed by 19 United States Senators and 77 Congressman, that urged resistance to implementation of the United States Supreme Court's school desegregation decision in *Brown v. Board of Education of Topeka, Kansas.*

The manifesto charged that *Brown* was an abuse of judicial power and a threat to destroy the public education system of the South. The list of senators and representatives who did not sign the manifesto was significant. Senators Lyndon B. Johnson of Texas, Albert Gore of Tennessee, and Estes Kefauver of Tennessee, and 24 Congressmen from southern states did not agree with the manifesto and would not sign the document.

Black historian John Hope Franklin, a native of Rentiesville, Oklahoma, and one of the leading historians of the twentieth century, partially blamed the Southern Manifesto on the chaos that often surrounded school desegregation:

> . . . it set the stage and tone for the resistance that followed during the next decade or so. The search for alternatives to desegregated schools led to a veritable spate of maneuvers ranging from pupil placement to the closing of some public schools and the establishment of private all white schools. The path of massive resistance led to the establishment of white citizens' councils and violent confrontations with blacks who had resorted to various forms of protest and demonstration against noncompliance with the decisions of their communities.[2]

In February, 1956, Stewart and other state NAACP leaders were called to an emergency meeting in Atlanta, Georgia. The call came from NAACP Special Counsel Thurgood Marshall, "At Atlanta we hope to agree upon an overall program of legal action on a state by state basis. We will prepare a legal blueprint of action for pending and future desegregation cases."[3]

Stewart was Marshall's constant companion at the Atlanta meeting, a fact chronicled by *New Yorker Magazine* writer Bernard Taper who was assigned to accompany Marshall to Atlanta.

Stewart was described in a lengthy article in the *New Yorker* as "a slight, jaunty, tea-colored man."[4]

The black leaders met at the Wheat Street Baptist Church. The *New Yorker* correspondent, the only white person among 50 men and women at the meeting, sat by Stewart on folding metal chairs as the conference began. Reverend James Hinton of South Carolina was chosen as timekeeper to make certain that none of the representatives exceeded the 15 minutes allocated each state to discuss the progress of desegregation.

The meeting was chaired by Marshall and Roy Wilkins. When the list of states present was read, Oklahoma was overlooked. When Reverend Hinton said, "What about Oklahoma?" Stewart looked up and said, "Oklahoma's been doin' so well we're practically a Northern state, and I wasn't sure you Southerners would want me at your meetin'." Stewart's comment drew laughter, one of the few light moments in the very serious meeting about the future of American school desegregation.

Stewart stood before the group and reported on Oklahoma school desegregation which he described as "smoother than he ever thought possible." Stewart reported that "not only had all school segregation ended in Oklahoma City but all race restrictions had been removed from the city's golf courses, municipal auditoriums, public buildings, some movie theaters, and from the state parks.

The *New Yorker* described the reports from the various states as detailed and factual, and presented in an unemotional and businesslike way, with state spokesmen giving information about the attitudes and actions of governmental officials, about petitions filed with school boards and the responses to them, about negotiations conducted, and about lawsuits, current or contemplated.

There was "intense absorption" by the listeners when the "ebullient Stewart" gave the Oklahoma report. The magazine reporter called Stewart's positive report on desegregation in Oklahoma less than boastful, "even his exuberance was free from any suggestion of gloating. Indeed, what he sounded most like was a chamber of commerce booster."[5]

After all the state representatives reported, attorney Marshall took over the meeting and led a discussion of what next to do. The group concluded that desegregation was satisfactorily progressing in Oklahoma, Delaware, Maryland, West Virginia, and Missouri, and that leaders in those states should watch vigilantly to make certain that the law of the land was followed.

Marshall identified a new problem, the vast number of black teachers who were fired as the result of consolidation of schools. Marshall urged steps be taken to ensure that professional qualifications and seniority, not race, be the deciding factor in determining which teachers would be dismissed. Marshall warned, "We must not allow the burden of racial discrimination to fall on the teachers now that it's been lifted from the students."[6]

"All right, listen to this statement. Jimmy's going to read," Marshall said after the conferees at the Atlanta meeting drafted a resolution recognizing areas of progress and deciding what legal action needed to be taken. Stewart read the handwritten document aloud, stumbling over some of the words. When he finished, someone said the statement certainly needed to be edited. Stewart said, "I don't know whether the errors were in the writing or the reading." Marshall replied, "I know at least one was in the reading."[7]

Wilkins, who had been relatively quiet during the meeting, strode to the front of the room and addressed the black leaders. "I don't believe we understand the tremendous effect we are having on the nation," he began. "All these little decisions we worked out today are part of a social revolution that is taking place. The whole face of America is changing—and what is achieved here in the South will also help to enhance the status of those who live outside the area and bring all of them closer to that condition we speak of so glibly in the phrase 'first-class citizenship.' "[8]

Stewart returned to Oklahoma City after the meeting and met with the local NAACP board. Everyone present at the meeting agreed that the Oklahoma City Board of Education and the school superintendent were saying the right words in promising to fully desegregate the public schools. In fact, technically, the schools were desegregated, a black student could go to any school in the area where he or she lived. However, Stewart wondered if true integration in the schools would ever take place. He would have to wait another decade to find out for sure.

In 1956 Stewart took a young Douglass High School football player under his wing. Prentice Gautt was captain of the 1955-1956 Douglass team, the best high school football player in the state, and an excellent college prospect. However, Gautt was not officially recruited by the university he wanted to attend, the University of Oklahoma.

Gautt received a break when he was allowed to play in the 1956 state high school all-star game, a first for black athletes in Oklahoma. He scored three touchdowns and was named the game's most valuable player. Gautt was elated when OU All-American Kurt Burris came up to him after the game and encouraged him to attend OU.

Stewart talked with OU Coach Bud Wilkinson who promised to consider giving an athletic scholarship to Gautt if he could pay his own tuition for the first semester and make the football team. Stewart helped Gautt make application to several organizations for academic scholarships. Within days the young football player was awarded a scholarship by the Oklahoma City Medical, Dental, and Pharmaceutical Association, a group of black professionals.

Life on the OU campus was tough for Gautt. Integration was proceeding slowly and Gautt was the first black athlete admitted to the university. As a walk-on without a scholarship, Gautt had to work his way into the hearts of the coaching staff.

When Gautt became discouraged, his fellow white players came to the rescue. On the way to a freshman game with the University of Tulsa, the team stopped to eat at a restaurant. The white players were outraged when a waitress refused to serve Gautt. Several players, including Brewster Hobby, Jim Davis, and Jere Durham, walked out.

Gautt practiced hard and made the team in his sophomore

Stewart was instrumental in the admission of Prentice Gautt to the University of Oklahoma where Gautt starred on the gridiron and paved the way for black athletes at the university. (Courtesy *The Daily Oklahoman*.)

year. As promised, Coach Wilkinson gave him a full athletic scholarship. Only a vocal minority of team members objected to a black man being part of the OU team.

After a terrible few days of practice in which team spirit was at an all-time low, Wilkinson confronted his team. He insisted that if the players were real men, they would have the guts to say to Gautt's face what they were saying about him behind his back. Wilkinson walked out of the meeting. Gautt arose and said he did not want to be a detriment to the team and also walked out.

Team captain Leon Cross led a team meeting in which it was decided that Gautt was an integral part of the OU program. The meeting solidified the team.

Gautt needed a summer job between semesters to earn spending money not supplied by his OU athletic scholarship. Stewart talked to Oklahoma City businessman John Kirkpatrick who gave Gautt a $10-a-day job on his farm near Yukon.

Gautt plowed new ground in black-white relations, especially when the OU team traveled. When OU played the University of Texas, Gautt was forced to stay in a different Dallas hotel than the white players. Even in Oklahoma City, the Skirvin Hotel refused to accommodate the team because of Gautt's presence. OU officials simply found another Oklahoma City hotel for the team to stay in on the nights before big games in Norman.[9]

Later Wilkinson said helping Gautt through his All-American years at OU was the single most significant thing he did in coaching. Gautt went on to professional football and held a high-ranking administrative job at the Big Eight Conference headquarters in Kansas City, Missouri, for many years.

In later years when Stewart attended OU games and saw the on-the-field exploits of stars like Joe Washington; Greg Pruitt; and Lucius, LeRoy, and Dewey Selmon, he quietly smiled, knowing he had played a part in the admission of black athletes to the University of Oklahoma.

In 1957 Stewart renewed his acquaintance with a Baptist minister in Alabama whose home had been bombed the previous year to protest his civil rights activities. Dr. Martin Luther King, Jr. and

60 other mostly black Baptist ministers had recently organized a new organization, the Southern Christian Leadership Conference (SCLC). Most of the preachers were members of their local NAACP branches but believed a collateral group was necessary to achieve quicker results with nonviolent social action.

King successfully led a bus boycott in his hometown of Montgomery, Alabama, and was elected the first president of the SCLC. He met with Stewart and other NAACP leaders in Atlanta to discuss a march in Washington, D.C. Many black leaders were irritated by the Eisenhower administration's failure to address civil rights issues, or to even meet with them.

Stewart, Roy Wilkins, and A. Philip Randolph publicly supported the SCLC which took the lead in promoting a "Prayer Pilgrimage to Washington," the first of the civil rights movement's five marches on Washington between 1957 and 1968. In the call for blacks to take part in the pilgrimage, a joint letter signed by Wilkins, Randolph, and King was widely distributed. In part, the letter was an invitation for blacks to become more active:

> We invite all believers in the God-given concept of the brotherhood of man and in the American ideal of equality, to assemble, review the national scene, give thanks for the progress to date, and pray for the wiping out of the evils that still beset our nation. . . We believe Americans are deeply religious and wish to order their lives and their country according to the great moral truths to be found in our common religious heritage. . . As the Founding Americans prayed for strength and wisdom in the wilderness of a new land, as the slaves and their descendants prayed for emancipation and human dignity. . . so we now, in these troubled and momentous years, call upon all who love justice and dignity and liberty, who love their country, and who love mankind, to join in a Prayer Pilgrimage.[10]

The Prayer Pilgrimage was held May 17, 1957, on the third anniversary of the Supreme Court's *Brown v. Board of Education of Topeka, Kansas* decision. Randolph, a black labor leader who founded the Brotherhood of Pullman Car Porters and Maids Union, presided over the event in Washington. Stewart joined a crowd that was estimated at 25,000, a small start for the giant crowds that would eventually converge on the nation's capital to express support for civil rights reform in America.

The Prayer Pilgrimage featured performances by Mahalia Jackson, Harry Belafonte, and Sammy Davis, Jr. and speeches by Roy Wilkins, New York Congressman Adam Clayton Powell, and King on the steps of the Lincoln Memorial.

The Prayer Pilgrimage drew attention to the American Civil Rights movement. The Eisenhower administration joined with leaders in Congress to create the Civil Rights Act of 1957 which established the United States Civil Rights Commission and included new guarantees of voting rights for minorities. President Eisenhower signed the act into law September 9, 1957.

Back home in Oklahoma City, Stewart turned his attention to minority representation on the city council. The capital city's population had shifted and the city charter demanded that new ward boundaries be drawn to equalize the population represented by each council member.

Stewart headed a delegation of black leaders who appeared at a series of meetings with the city council. Stewart spoke for the Citizens Action Committee, a group of 30 black organizations. Stewart asked the council to add at least one new ward to the existing four wards. His reason was simple. If a new ward was created that contained most of the black voters, the chances of a black man or woman being elected to the city council would be greatly enhanced.

Stewart denied accusations that blacks "wanted a ward of their own."[11] Instead, Stewart argued, keeping most blacks in one ward would make their voices heard better at city hall, "We just want to be in a position to make our needs felt, regardless of who is representing us."[12]

Stewart's efforts to add at least one ward to the city boundary configuration failed, even though he convinced Mayor Allen Street to support such a plan. Over the mayor's objection, the city council approved a plan to re-draw boundary lines but retain only the four existing wards. A newspaper described Stewart's comments at the council meeting "splendid but futile."[13] After the meeting, Stewart pledged to work for the defeat of Ward Two councilman Bob Constant who had supported the plan which, in Stewart's opinion, was obviously geared to dilute the strength of the black vote. Even though defeated for the moment, Stewart did not give up hope that someday a black man or woman could serve on the city council of Oklahoma City.

THIRTEEN
INTO THE STREETS

Stewart called the year 1957 "a year of decision" in his annual report to the Oklahoma City Branch of the NAACP. That was a monumental understatement.

The civil rights struggle across the South was riding a new level of intensity. Opposition to discriminatory laws or action, previously limited to court action, was moved to the streets by a new spirit of activism. Even though court actions slowed protests in Texas, Louisiana and Alabama, Stewart was optimistic about the future of the civil rights movement:

> Our foreparents during the days of slavery used to sing a song, "God Moves of the Waters." and from the reports we get daily from Montgomery, Birmingham, Tallahassee and other places, God is moving in the hearts and minds of many who formerly could not see the light of righteousness and fair play so far as their Negro brothers were concerned. And might I say much of this action stems directly from God's church and men of God such as those noble ministers in those cities. Men and women of good will cannot let them bear this cross alone.[1]

Some of the 85 black youths who waited on service at John A. Brown's lunch counter in August, 1958. (Courtesy *The Daily Oklahoman*.)

Stewart challenged Oklahoma City blacks with nine goals for the NAACP in 1957. His program included giving blacks an equal chance for a good job, protecting black lives against mob violence, securing the right to vote without fear, complete desegregation of public schools, abolition of Jim Crow in all modes of transportation, total access and use of all public facilities, desegregation of private and public housing, assuring an equal opportunity for members of the national guard and the armed forces, and building a stronger local chapter of the Youth Council, the NAACP program to attract children and teenagers to the organization[2].

In the annual report, Stewart said a Youth Council had been sponsored in previous years in name only, "We have never really invested heavily in building a youth movement as it should be. This year, this must be done."[3] Stewart launched a search for volunteers to assist in an active Youth Council, whose activities over the next decade would make headlines and history.

A summer trip to New York City by a group of Oklahoma City black teenagers from the Youth Council in 1957 spawned a series

of events that changed the face of the American civil rights movement. And Stewart was right in the middle of the action.

The only volunteer to become an adult advisor to the Youth Council was Clara Luper, a history teacher at Dunjee High School. A native of rural Okfuskee County, and a graduate of Langston University, Luper reorganized the Youth Council in January, 1957. William Miles was elected president of the group. Luper was given the title of Youth Advisor. From that position Luper quickly established herself as a new-style aggressive leader in the struggle for equality in Oklahoma.

Luper believed strongly in the non-violent methods of protest preached by Dr. Martin Luther King, Jr. She was so moved by his leadership, she wrote a play, "Brother President," about King's protests in Alabama for presentation during Negro History Week.

In May, 1957, Luper led 26 members of the local Youth Council on a trip to New York City to stage the play at the national NAACP convention. The group traveled through Ohio and Pennsylvania and were shocked to receive regular service at lunch counters and restaurants. It was a new experience for Oklahoma City black teenagers to eat at the same counter with whites.

On their return trip, Luper and her Youth Council members took the southern route, again encountering humiliating discrimination. Luper decided during the trip to ask the senior leaders of the local NAACP to support her fight to integrate Oklahoma City's eating establishments. Luper recognized that integration had already taken place, without incident, in schools, on buses, and in theaters and amusement parks. She thought, "If we can play golf and ride the bus with whites, why can't we eat with them?"

Luper presented her bold plan to Stewart and the Executive Committee of the Oklahoma City Branch of the NAACP. Stewart believed that the best approach was through quiet negotiation. After all, that was the method that had succeeded in integrating other public places in Oklahoma over the previous five years.

Stewart recommended, and the Executive Committee agreed, that the Youth Council send its members, in groups of three, to talk to restaurant owners about opening up their serving areas to blacks. The visits began in May, 1957, and did not catch the attention of the press.

The teenagers were instructed to dress nicely and make their pitch for equal treatment in a dignified and pleasant way. Stewart, Luper, and other leaders met with city officials to request a city ordinance banning segregation in public accommodations. City leaders responded, "We are sorry, we do not have the power to interfere in private businesses. We don't tell the businessmen who to serve and they don't tell us how to run our city government."[4]

The quiet negotiation tactic failed miserably. Luper began mapping plans, with the approval of Stewart and the NAACP, to eliminate segregation in eating establishments by physically protesting the discrimination. Stewart's first advice to Luper was that children and teenagers, not adults, be used in the protests. Stewart reasoned that whites would tolerate the actions of protesting black children more than black adults. Stewart encouraged his children, Jimmy, Jr. and Zandra, to participate in the protests led by Luper.

Luper's theory of non-violence was drilled into the minds of Youth Council members. Luper believed, "The doctrine of non-violence is rooted in the fundamental truth that whites are human. Being human, they will probably react with fear if they are threatened, but in the final analysis, they are likely to respond with good will. The white man's reaction may be one of surprise because we are not answering injustices with injustices."[5]

Luper taught her students to love their enemies, keep their goal of desegregation in sight, and to give the white man a way out, "Recognize that he has weaknesses and can be embarrassed for mistreating his brother. Find a way to let him participate in victory when it comes."[6]

Luper focused on five major lunch counters in downtown Oklahoma City, John A. Brown Department Store, Veazey's Drug, Kress, Green's Variety Store, and Katz Drug, as targets for one of the first "sit-in" demonstrations in the South. A few weeks earlier, students in Wichita, Kansas, quietly protested at a restaurant without incident or publicity.

Stewart, as leader of the local NAACP branch, gave the Youth Council guidelines to govern activities during protests of the lunch counters:

> Avoid any situation which would place them in the position of disturbing the peace; select one spokesman and direct all inquiries to that person; carry no weapons, don't chew gum, don't laugh when the other fellow does things which may amuse you under normal circumstances because your task was a serious matter and a little innocent laugh may irritate our opposition and cause unfavorable reactions; above all, don't engage in name calling and don't strike back if attacked since there would be sufficient police at all times to give protection.[7]

On August 19, 1958, more than a year after negotiations had failed to integrate eating establishments, Luper led thirteen youngsters, from age five to fifteen, including her own two children, to Katz Drug on the southwest corner of Main and Robinson streets. Katz had a first-class pharmacy, a gift and toy shop, and a lunch counter. Blacks were allowed to shop in the store and could even order sandwiches and drinks to go. Blacks were simply prohibited from eating their meals at the lunch counter.

Fifteen-year-old Barbara Posey, a member of the Youth Council, approached the counter and ordered 13 Coca-Colas. The frightened red-faced manager rushed to Luper and said, "Mrs. Luper, you know better than this. You know we don't serve colored folks at the counter."[8]

Luper and her 13 demonstrators did not back down, even though policemen surrounded them within minutes. The Katz sit-in was the first of many in Oklahoma City and signaled a long period of unprecedented activism for Oklahoma City blacks.

The management of Green's Variety Store and Veazey's Drug agreed to serve blacks without a sit-in. However, other downtown lunch counters resisted.

Luper and her youthful demonstrators protested at Katz Drug for three days. From there the group moved to the Kress lunch counter where they were served, but in an unusual way. The management had removed the counter stools so the sit-in participants had to stand to drink their Coca-Colas.[9]

Stewart and other black leaders supported Luper and the sit-in demonstrations but wondered out loud if it was proper to use youngsters for the protests. Reverend W. K. Jackson, pastor of St. John's Missionary Baptist Church at Second and Phillips streets since 1945, was concerned that the youths might be hurt. After the first few sit-ins, Jackson, a native of Boley, Oklahoma, and president of the powerful Oklahoma Black Baptist Ministers Convention, threw his wholehearted support behind Luper and even organized a group of black preachers who chauffeured the demonstrators to the hundreds of sit-ins and protest marches that would be held in Oklahoma City.

The downtown lunch counter that was most resistant to change was at the John A. Brown store. Luper and her group tried unsuccessfully to be served at the Brown's counter for several days. Brown's was the largest department store in the state and Luper could not understand how the company encouraged blacks to shop in its store but would not serve them food at the lunch counter.

Luper received daily threats from people opposed to her role in the sit-in demonstrations. Threats included a sack of shotgun shells left on her front porch, hate mail, and a promise to bomb her house.

However, not all whites opposed the NAACP's efforts to integrate eating places in Oklahoma City. The *Oklahoma City Times* "Friday Forum" contained hundreds of letters in 1958 from whites who supported the sit-in demonstrations. The black community was solidly behind the protests. Eugene D. Jones, Jr., a black resident of Oklahoma City, wrote, "Hurrah to the Negro Youths who brought to light the shame and disgrace that Oklahoma City has hidden and overlooked for these many years. Hurrah for the white youths who are showing more Christianity and intelligence than their predecessors by asking for a logical reason for being prejudiced."[10] William E. Byerly expressed the thinking of many whites,

"It is essential for us in the churches to demonstrate that we foster a community transcending all differences of race, sex, nationality and social or political affiliation. Thanks to the fine spirit of our Negro youths and the attitude of many local business people in helping to rectify old sores and bad practices."[11]

The veiled anonymity of the newspaper's "Friday Forum" allowed bigoted members of the community to criticize the NAACP for using "mere children" to advance the cause of civil rights. One letter printed by the *Times* was filled with hate and racial prejudice, "Just like groups led by Hitler and Stalin, the NAACP is not satisfied. They want more. Now they want to sit and eat with us. This is the last hurdle in Oklahoma. Once they get through it, the next thing you know, your sons and daughters will be bringing home colored wives and husbands."[12]

From around the state, whites began to vocalize their support for equality. A Seminole resident wrote, "When are people going to wake up and realize that Negroes were born here. It isn't fair that they should fight for this country in time of need, and then have to fight for their very existence when they return home."[13] From Purcell, Oklahoma, businessman George M. Jenks declared his support for Luper and the sit-in movement and pledged to "deny patronage to any establishment that refuses service on an equal basis to Negroes and whites."[14]

Luper later described the protest at John A. Brown's as the "Bunker Hill" of the sit-in movement. Luper wrote, "The sit-ins at Brown's were just like a splash in a summer pool. They became like a tornado on a quiet, cloudy spring day. They were now bringing fear to the white community and a new kind of fear and respect to the black community."[15]

The protest at Brown's escalated, with as many as 100 blacks, including Stewart's own children Jimmy, Jr. and Zandra, showing up for the daily attempt at service. Still, Brown's refused to serve blacks. As interest in the protests waned, Luper suspended the sit-ins in September. Stewart renewed his efforts to talk privately with store owners to accomplish the public goal of integrating public accommodations in Oklahoma City.[16]

Four of the five targets of Luper's 1958 sit-in campaign integrated their lunch counters. A dozen other eating places also opened their doors to blacks without sit-ins.

Luper and her group received nationwide publicity. The *New York Times* printed no fewer than five major stories on the Oklahoma City protest. National NAACP leaders pointed to the peaceful element of the protests as a model for other blacks planning public demonstrations in the South. Oklahoma City was in direct contrast with Montgomery, Alabama, where Dr. Martin Luther King, Jr. was arrested, jailed, and kicked by police a few days after the sit-in at Katz Drug.

The success of Luper and the sit-ins drew a young black attorney back to Oklahoma. E. Melvin Porter, a native of Okmulgee, Oklahoma, turned down offers in other states and returned to his roots to practice law. Tulsa attorney Amos Hall advanced Porter sufficient money to set up a law office on Second Street in Oklahoma City. Porter immediately began to assist Luper as an advisor to the Youth Council.

In 1959, only a few formal sit-ins were conducted by the Youth Council. Instead brief student protests during lunch hours were made at dozens of eating places such as the Anna Maude Cafeteria and Bishop's Restaurant. Blacks often asked, "May we eat today?" The answer was usually no. Ralph Adair, owner of Adair's Cafeteria, refused service blacks because he believed he would lose all his white customers if he caved in to Luper's demands.[17]

In March, 1959, Stewart appeared before the city council along with representatives of the Oklahoma City Council of Churches to ask again for the passage of an ordinance outlawing segregation in public accommodations. The council refused, agreeing with the city attorney that the council lacked the power to pass such an ordinance.

Stewart grew in stature in his role as a national board member of the NAACP. At the 1959 national convention, the 50th anniversary convention, Stewart was vice chairman of the convention Steering Committee. He spent months before the convention coordinating the massive schedule for the July event. Stewart was elected chairman of the Freedom Fund Dinner Committee.

Stewart turned over the reins of the Oklahoma City Branch of the NAACP in 1959 to a young black dentist, Dr. E. C. Moon, Jr., the nephew of legendary black educator F. D. Moon and son of a prominent Oklahoma City physician. In passing the baton to Moon, Stewart said it was time to give new leadership a chance, "for the battle is still to be won."[18] In early 1960, frustrated with the lack of movement by restaurant owners, Stewart, Luper and other black leaders planned a massive sit-in to be held at the John A. Brown store downtown. However, Oklahoma Governor J. Howard Edmondson asked that the demonstration be called off to give him a chance to appoint a Governor's Committee on Human Relations to work on the specific problem of lunch counter segregation and other issues of integration.

In March, Edmondson announced the formation of the statewide committee. Its 30 members included Oklahoma City physician and Urban League President Dr. Charles Atkins, banker Harvey Everest, Episcopal Bishop Chilton Powell, newspaper editor Charles Bennett, banker John Rogers, Oklahoma City University President Dr. Jack Wilkes, Reverend Ben Hill, Reverend W. K. Jackson, Douglass High School Principal F. D. Moon, Wayne B. Snow, president of the Council of Churches, popular Oklahoma City minister Dr. W. McFerrin Stowe, Luper, and Stewart, who was appointed to the legal committee and food service, hotel, and motel accommodations sub-committees. Governor Edmondson said, "While Oklahoma has made good progress toward ending racial segregation, I am convinced that more can and should be done to achieve further progress in this direction."[19]

Stewart was a strong supporter of Edmondson and the statewide committee. He believed that if the committee would take a definitive stand against segregation and discrimination, "the people will accept it."

Immediately, there was a difference of opinion among black leaders as to whether the massive demonstration planned for Brown's should be canceled. Luper was in Washington, D.C. mobilizing outside support for the demonstration. She, and most members of the Youth Council, were firmly against canceling the Brown's protest. Luper was livid when she arrived back in Oklahoma City and learned that Stewart, and the Executive Committee of the NAACP, had agreed to cancel the Brown's demonstration to give Edmondson a chance to resolve the sticky issues surrounding the segregation question.

Stewart and the senior branch of the NAACP took some of the limelight away from the Youth Council and its desegregation efforts. Often tensions developed between the younger and older NAACP members. However, Stewart and Luper kept the lines of communication open and stressed the absolute necessity of unity in the black community.[20]

Edmondson, at age 33, was the state's youngest governor. He demonstrated his progressive attitude by appointing the Committee on Human Relations. However, observers believed that Edmondson also was afraid of violence impacting Oklahoma's image and the successful industrial development campaign he instituted.

One of the first projects of the Committee on Human Relations was to survey Oklahoma City businesses that had integrated to prove the point that there would be no economic loss for other restaurant owners who chose to serve blacks.

Negotiations again failed to convince white restaurant owners to serve blacks. Governor Edmondson met personally with owners and managers of lunch counters and restaurants. Edmondson appealed for integration because of justice and fairness and because he believed the publicity was detrimental to the city and state. Edmondson's pleas went unheeded. Integration of public accommodations in Oklahoma City was at a stalemate.[21]

Oklahoma City received less than favorable national publicity in April, 1960, when professional football star Jim Brown was denied room accommodations at major hotels and motels in the city. Brown, who worked for the Pepsi-Cola Company in the off season was forced to stay at the Fourth Street YMCA. Stewart was embarrassed for both Brown, Pepsi-Cola, and Oklahoma City.

In July, 1960, black leaders saw no results from continuing negotiations with restaurant owners. Blacks were restless. Luper and others proposed a boycott of all downtown Oklahoma City businesses unless every eating establishment opened its doors to blacks. White business and civic leaders tried to convince black leaders that the economic boycott would hurt the black cause.

Stewart, Dr. Atkins, and optometrist Dr. A. L. Dowell were among moderate leaders who wanted to postpone the boycott to give Edmondson's Human Relations Committee more time to work on the problem. Luper; dentist Dr. E. C. Moon, Jr.; Porter; and Cecil Williams, Stewart's successor as president of the Oklahoma City NAACP Branch, vehemently argued that nothing else but a boycott would force downtown businesses to open their lunch counters to blacks.

Stewart and his supporters prevailed. The boycott was postponed pending further negotiations between Human Relations Committee and restaurant owners. Almost daily some member of the governor's committee conferred with downtown merchants. Nothing, including newspaper advertisements signed by hundreds of white citizens who supported desegregation, and the support of the Roman Catholic and Jewish congregations, could change the mind of downtown restaurant owners.

On August 5, Dr. Martin Luther King, Jr., by then an icon and the most visible civil rights leader in the country, addressed 2,000 people gathered in Oklahoma City for a meeting of the Oklahoma City Negro Baptist Ministers Association at The Calvary Baptist Church at Second and Walnut streets. He said, "The Negro wants his freedom, and he wants his freedom now. The Negro has come to re-evaluate himself and has come to feel that he is somebody."[22]

King, in his only public appearance in Oklahoma City in his life that would be shortened by an assassin's bullet eight years later, stressed the need for being prepared, the substitution of love for hate, the advocacy of peaceful demonstrations as a successful means of action. King said, "We who live in the 20th century have the privilege of standing between the two ages—the dying old and the emerging new."[23]

With his unique preaching style, King told the Oklahoma City black community that he supported the proposed boycott of downtown businesses. King's approval of the boycott, strongly cheered by the crowd, may have been the turning point in the community's split over the value of the general boycott.[24]

After King spoke, Stewart, Dr. Charles Atkins, Reverend J.C. West, and Barbara Posey of the NAACP Youth Council gave three-minute speeches on the importance of banding together in the fight for civil rights.

After the mass rally, in a private meeting, King urged Stewart, Luper, and other black leaders to back the boycott of downtown merchants because of the success of similar actions in Alabama and Georgia.

The Black Dispatch announced its support of the boycott in its August 19th edition, "The spirit of Frederick Douglass and the 40-year crusade of Roscoe Dunjee still rests in the hearts, minds and souls of black people in Oklahoma and we are behind them as well as with them in any movement within the American credo toward the fulfillment of that dream. No one will do this for us, we must do it for and among ourselves."[25] The newspaper's stand on the boycott issue was important to voices in the black community demanding immediate action.

A crucial meeting of the black community was held August 19 at St. John's Missionary Baptist Church on Second Street. Stewart, Dr. Atkins, and Herbert Wright, a national NAACP official, all argued that a general boycott was unfair to the businesses who already served blacks.

In a tense moment, E. Melvin Porter took the floor, and while "running his right hand through his curly hair and frowns covering his face," spoke in a "thunderous, steady voice, his words falling like Oklahoma's April thunderstorms." Porter called those against the boycott Uncle Toms and Aunt Jemimas.[26]

A loud roar greeted the introduction of Clara Luper. The only choice was to boycott, she said. "Some blacks would say 'Give them more time.' Time for what? The clock on the wall says the time is now. We will wear old clothes and walk with new dignity."[27]

Luper quoted Dr. King, "we must refuse to cooperate with segregation." When the crowd grew restless as the various speakers propounded their theories either for or against the boycott, it was Rubye Hall who pleaded for unity. In the end, the frustration with long, fruitless negotiations convinced blacks at the meeting that a general boycott was the only answer. Hundreds of adults volunteered to carry picket signs. The boycott was slated to begin August 22, with nine previously desegregated restaurants exempt.

The boycott lasted 11 months. Luper tactfully organized a series of sit-ins to place emphasis on the boycott. Actor Charlton Heston led a May, 1961, anti-segregation march through the streets of downtown Oklahoma City. The boycott ended in July, 1961, after Harvey Everest, Chairman of the Governor's Committee on Human Relations, announced that John A. Brown, the Forum Cafeteria, and H. L. Green would serve blacks. The opening of Brown's was considered a significant victory.

There was a difference of opinion on what impact the boycott had. Stewart was convinced that the fact that 115 restaurants had opened their doors to blacks was proof certain that businesses felt the crunch of the economic boycott. On the other hand, merchants claimed the boycott had little impact. A police officer who was on hand for many of the demonstrations said business owners finally gave in because of the fear of violence that was occurring in protests in other parts of the United States.[28]

The first arrests during the sit-ins in Oklahoma City occurred in January, 1961, when demonstrators seeking service at Anna Maude's Cafeteria in the Cravens Building were hauled off to jail.

The Anna Maude Cafeteria demonstration was significant because whites began to join Oklahoma City blacks in the protest against discrimination. Father Robert G. McDole, assistant pastor at Corpus Christi Catholic Church, and Reverend John Heidbrink, a chaplain at Oklahoma City University, joined in the protest.

Demonstrations were necessary for the next few years until blacks could eat at any place in Oklahoma City. But Clara Luper and the NAACP Youth Council had begun an historic trend that could not be stopped.

FOURTEEN
MORE PROTESTS

WITH THE ELECTION OF JOHN F. KENNEDY as President of the United States in 1960, the civil rights movement gained a friend, and the pendulum of change in America swung closer to racial equality. Kennedy was the first American president to openly condemn segregation as a moral wrong.

The aggressive campaign to shed the spotlight of justice and equality on the wrongs inflicted on black Americans was working. John Hope Franklin wrote:

> The drive to destroy the two worlds of race has reached a new, dramatic, and somewhat explosive stage in recent years. The forces arrayed in behalf of maintaining these two worlds have been subjected to ceaseless and powerful attacks by the increasing numbers committed to the elimination of racism in American life. Through techniques of demonstrating, picketing, sitting-in, and boycotting they have not only harassed their foes but marshaled their forces.[1]

Stewart, as a national board member of the NAACP, subscribed to the theory of Roy Wilkins and Thurgood Marshall that legislation was needed to guarantee the civil rights of all people, to eliminate employment discrimination, and to finally achieve livable public and private housing for poor blacks and whites.

President Kennedy made substantial campaign promises regarding civil rights during the months preceding the 1960 election. After his election, Kennedy quickly moved to increase the federal government's role in promoting equality through integration. In March, 1961, the President signed Executive Order 10925, creating the Equal Employment Opportunity Commission. The commission, chaired by Vice President Lyndon B. Johnson, was essentially a committee of the president's cabinet which was responsible for eliminating discrimination based on color, national origin, race or religion in union membership and employment by the government or government contractors. The commission later was made a federal agency by the Civil Rights Act of 1964.

Back in Oklahoma City, sit-in demonstrations continued. However, the focus changed from downtown restaurants to eating establishments all over the capital city. The resolve of the NAACP and its Youth Council was rewarded with a more responsive city government that began to use its power to work toward equality.

Stewart, F. D. Moon and other black leaders again recommended passage of a city ordinance to outlaw segregation in public accommodations. Some white leaders argued that no ordinance was necessary because many businesses had abandoned old segregation practices. Stewart declared, "As long as there is one business that won't serve blacks, we need the principle of equality written into law."[2] The City Council again tabled the issue.

In the early 1960s many white homeowners feared blacks moving into their neighborhoods would cause property values to plummet. When whites began leaving residential areas north of Northeast Twenty-third Street between Eastern and Santa Fe avenues, the NAACP was accused of pushing blacks to move into all-white neighborhoods, a charge Stewart denied. He told a newspaper reporter that the NAACP did not provide "one dime" toward purchase of housing by blacks nor did the organization give advice on where blacks should live.[3]

Northeast Twenty-third Street was the unofficial boundary line of where blacks should live, according to many whites concerned that neighborhoods, and neighborhood elementary schools north of that line, would be quickly and permanently integrated.

Vestal J. Vaughn, drycleaner and president of the Northeast Oklahoma City Chamber of Commerce, a predominantly white organization, attempted to diffuse the panic selling in white neighborhoods by instituting an information campaign.

Stewart promoted the idea of better housing for blacks. He advocated a slum clearance program and the opening of new additions for blacks who could afford new homes. Stewart blamed the migration of blacks into white neighborhoods on the serious shortage of good, middle-class homes in traditionally all-black areas.

The *Oklahoma City Times* agreed with Stewart's statements about the need for improved housing. An editorial entitled "Commendable Action" said, "The attitudes of spokesmen for both the white and Negro groups in the matter of a possible real estate 'block busting' [the practice of placing a black family in a white neighborhood to lower property values] stampede on the northeast side is to be commended. Action by civic leaders to initiate slum clearance and plan for new additions suitable to the needs of Negroes who can pay the price is a good step."[4]

Stewart, no longer president of the local NAACP branch, formed a new organization called Oklahomans for Progress. Stewart was totally supportive of NAACP programs, but wanted his new organization, made up of black and white leaders from all over the state who were sympathetic to his causes, to be an independent voice for change. Stewart was quick to point out that his new group did not intend to be a substitution or elimination of any organized group.

Stewart tapped his old friends F. D. Moon, H. C. Whitlow, and A. L. Lipton to serve on the Executive Board of Oklahomans for Progress. Stewart intended the group to serve as sort of a clearing house or coordinating agency for many organized civil rights groups in the state with primary emphasis on legislation and enhancement of economic opportunities for minorities.[5]

Stewart's support of Democratic gubernatorial nominee W. P. "Bill" Atkinson in 1962 was acceptable to black Oklahomans but repulsed a leading NAACP official in New York. Grant Reynolds, president of the White Plains, New York Branch of the NAACP, demanded Stewart's resignation from the national NAACP Board of Directors in August, 1962. Reynolds sent a telegram to NAACP Executive Director Roy Wilkins, "It is inconceivable that Stewart could actively support any candidate for public office whose record reveals him to be completely at war with the objectives of our organization."[6] Reynolds was referring to covenants restricting blacks in some of the additions Atkinson built in Midwest City, covenants that existed in almost every development in Oklahoma County for the prior 25 years.

Stewart, who had actively supported Republicans Dwight Eisenhower in 1952 and 1956 and Richard Nixon in 1960, was true to his Democratic registration in the 1962 governor's race with his vocal support for Atkinson. He was incensed by Reynolds' call for his resignation.

In a letter to Wilkins, Stewart credited Atkinson with helping to integrate the hotel where Reynolds had stayed while campaigning for Republican candidates in Oklahoma City. Stewart reported that Atkinson, who also owned the Uptown Cafeteria, was one of the first Oklahoma City restaurant owners to serve blacks.[7]

Billings, Oklahoma, farmer Henry Bellmon was inaugurated as the state's first Republican governor in January, 1963, after defeating Atkinson in the general election.

Bellmon was sympathetic to the winds of change in race relations. He had refused to take part in a civil rights march in Oklahoma City in 1961 during the visit of actor Charlton Heston because he was in the middle of the campaign for governor. Bellmon feared his participation in the march would alienate large numbers of white voters. He told his black supporters that he could not help their cause as governor unless he first won the election.[8]

After Bellmon took office he pledged to press for desegregation of both state and privately-owned facilities. He demonstrated his sincerity by hiring a young black woman, Beulah Ponder, as the receptionist in the governor's office in the state capitol building, certainly a shock to many who had never seen much participation by blacks in the seat of state government.

PLEASE
USE OTHER
DOOR

Demonstrators wait at the door of Bishop's Restaurant in downtown Oklahoma City, August 5, 1960. (Courtesy *The Daily Oklahoman.*)

In early 1963, 20 black and white professionals formed an independent political organization known as the Association for Responsible Government (ARG) in Oklahoma City. The stated goal of the new group was to support candidates for city council who would run the city in a more professional manner and be more responsive to the will of the people.[10]

The ARG played a key role in the 1963 city council elections, taking control of the mayor's office and several council seats. Jack S. Wilkes, a Methodist minister and president of Oklahoma City University, was elected mayor in a campaign in which he publicly vowed to create more opportunities for minorities. The city council hired Robert Tinstman of Abilene, Texas, as city manager.

Tinstman recommended, and the council approved, the establishment of a Community Relations Committee to improve communications between police and the black community and to assure fair employment opportunities for blacks. The Committee was packed with the city's most well-known leaders such as Stewart, Dean McGee, Rabbi Joseph Levenson, Clara Luper, Stanley Draper, Joe Dodson, Harvey P. Everest, Eugene Mathews, E. Melvin Porter, Guy H. James, Dr. Charles Atkins, and Frank Carey, Jr.

The Community Relations Committee set about to develop reliable statistics on the plight of blacks in Oklahoma City. The findings revealed the pitiful employment status of blacks workers who comprised 11 percent of the total labor force but accounted for 25 percent of the total unemployed. There was a 45 percent gap in family income, $3,233 for black families compared to

Facing, above: In January, 1961, demonstrators were arrested for picketing at the Anna Maude Cafeteria. Here police wait on a patrol wagon to escort nine demonstrators to the police station where they were booked into jail on complaints of disorderly conduct. (Courtesy *The Daily Oklahoman*.)

Facing, below: Anti-segregation demonstrators sat and squatted on the floor in the lobby of the Skirvin Hotel in downtown Oklahoma City, June 24, 1961. (Courtesy *The Daily Oklahoman*.)

$5,835 for white families. In city government, only 310 blacks were employed in a work force of 2,513. More importantly, 252 of the 310 were laborers earning an average monthly salary of $260.[11]

City Manager Tinstman recognized the widespread discrimination against blacks in promotions for city jobs. Upon his request, the city council unanimously approved a new city personnel policy that prohibited racial discrimination.

The new city administration also took an active role in mediating disputes between blacks and restaurant owners who had dug in their heels against the nationwide trend toward total integration of the races.

In May, E. Melvin Porter led 20 chanting pickets in a demonstration outside the Central YMCA in downtown Oklahoma City. Stewart, a longtime supporter of the YMCA programs in Oklahoma City, called upon Claude Monnet, president of the YMCA board, to voluntarily allow blacks to rent rooms in the Y dormitory. Monnet refused, saying that the YMCA on Fourth Street was especially built for blacks.[12]

Demonstrations at the YMCA continued for several days. In less than a month, the YMCA board of management voted to integrate its dormitory facilities.

In early June, 1963, the Youth Council held daily sit-ins at the Skirvin Hotel restaurant and Bishop's Restaurant, two of the few segregation hold-outs. While Clara Luper and hundreds of demonstrators appeared at the restaurants, Stewart, Mayor Wilkes, and Frank Carey, Jr., chairman of the city's 15-member Community Relations Committee, met privately with restaurant owners. Negotiations were easier, and more fruitful, than in earlier years when white business owners feared economic ruin if they served blacks. That oft-predicted calamity never occurred. After the June sit-ins, and the behind-closed-doors negotiations, 20 more restaurants in Oklahoma City desegregated, including the Anna Maude Cafeteria, Bishop's Restaurant, and the Huckins Hotel restaurant.

Oklahoma City's two major amusement parks, Springlake and Wedgewood, were still segregated in 1963. Stewart, E. Melvin Porter, and Reverend W.K. Jackson met with Springlake management and worked out a plan for the park to admit blacks. Wedgewood was more difficult.

When Luper heard that Wedgewood owner Maurice Woods said he would not allow blacks to enter the park, Luper replied, "We've heard the word 'no' before."[13] On June 22, Luper led 50 black and white demonstrators to the gates of Wedgewood where they were met by owner Woods. Luper invited Woods to tell the demonstrators why he insisted on segregation for his park. Woods was honest and said it was not a moral question but was strictly financial. He said he had $2 million invested in the park and could not take a gamble that white patrons would stay away from his facility if he allowed blacks to enter at the same time.[14]

All 50 demonstrators were arrested after they refused Woods' demands to leave his property. Stewart, Luper, Porter, and members of the city's Community Relations Commission met into the night with Woods. The next morning Woods reversed himself and

Blacks could not rent rooms at the downtown Oklahoma City YMCA until 1963 protests convinced the Board of Directors to desegregate the facility. (Courtesy *The Daily Oklahoman*.)

Fifty demonstrators were arrested in a much-publicized attempt to desegregate Wedgewood Amusement Park, northwest Oklahoma City June 22, 1963. (Courtesy *Daily Oklahoman.*)

voluntarily integrated the park on the Northwest Highway. A few weeks later, with business thriving, Woods admitted he was wrong in his fears that the city would not support an integrated park.[15]

For some reason, Woods changed his mind again several weeks later, limiting blacks to mingle with whites only one day per week. Back came the NAACP Youth Council and more protests. After another round of meetings, Woods opened his doors to all people of all colors on all days.

Luper called a halt to sit-ins for almost six months. One reason was Oklahoma Governor Henry Bellmon's plan to establish a state Human Rights Commission to handle complaints and formulate policy to guarantee civil rights for all citizens. The state legislature quickly heeded Bellmon's call for the commission and enacted legislation in June creating the agency. Major William Rose was chosen as the agency's first Executive Director.

In August, 1963, Stewart traveled to Washington, D.C. for the "March on Washington," staged by the NAACP, Dr. Martin Luther King's Southern Christian Leadership Conference, and other civil rights organizations, to highlight the need for federal legislation to condemn segregation and equalize employment opportunities. Stewart and Luper led a delegation of 70 Oklahomans who were among more than 250,000 demonstrators who heard the famous "I Have a Dream" speech by King, which captured the mood of the civil rights movement. Stewart never forgot the congregation of blacks and whites, rich and poor, professionals and laborers, gathered at the Lincoln Memorial for as far as the eye could see.

King followed a prepared text for the first five minutes of his speech. However, when he paraphrased the prophet Amos, "We will not be satisfied until justice runs down like waters," he laid his papers aside and began to preach. He said, "Do not wallow in despair. . . Despite all the difficulties, I still have a dream. It is a dream deeply rooted in the American dream. I have a dream that one day this nation will rise up and live out the true meaning of its creed—we hold these truths to be self-evident, that all men are created equal."[16]

Stewart and others who attended the March on Washington returned to Oklahoma inspired and more determined than ever to win the battle for equality. Within three months, President Kennedy was assassinated in Dallas and the presidential duties fell to Vice President Johnson, who continued to encourage Congress to approve major civil rights legislation and declared the nation's first War on Poverty.

The Oklahoma City NAACP Youth Council's final push for desegregation came in November, 1963, when Calvin Luper, Clara Luper's son, called for action at the 1963 state NAACP convention, saying blacks must "demonstrate, demonstrate, and demonstrate with sit-ins, lay-ins, or smoke-ins to end segregation."[17] Sit-in tactics were renewed and the Youth Council began active protest against Ralph's Drug Store and the Split-T Restaurant.

The city council was the battleground in 1964 for the public accommodations segregation dispute. Stewart and other leaders appeared before the council in March with the draft of a strong public accommodations ordinance in hand. The Community Relations Committee fully supported the ordinance which would prohibit hotels, motels, cafeterias, restaurants, swimming pools, skating rinks, bowling alleys and retail stores from refusing to serve anyone because of race, religion, or color. The proposed ordinance provided for a $20 per day fine for violation and empowered the city council to declare a business a public nuisance and close it down for repeated violations.

Hotel, motel, and restaurant owners organized against the ordinance, arguing that the law gave the city too much power. Cooper Lyons, representing the Anna Maude Cafeteria, feared frivolous claims of discrimination would be used to harass businesses. Other restaurant owners insisted that the law was unnecessary because an overwhelming majority of eating places were already desegregated.

When the city council tabled the motion approving the ordinance, Luper led 40 demonstrators to the Split-T Restaurant at Grand and North Western avenues. Several arrests were made after Split-T management obtained a court-ordered injunction against the protest.

To demonstrate the NAACP's determination, another sit-in was held at Ned's Steak House. This time there were no arrests.

Finally, on June 2, 1964, the city council approved the public accommodations ordinance, after six years of sit-ins, boycotts, parades, and hundreds of hours of private negotiations. On July 3, Luper led a group of demonstrators to five restaurants to test the new law. The blacks were served in all locations. The battle was over.

Historian John Henry Lee Thompson gave partial credit for the Oklahoma City success at ending desegregation in public accommodations to the media, "Media coverage of sit-ins, boycotts,

Stewart, right, with Oklahoma United States Senator Henry Bellmon, center, and Mamie Jackson. Bellmon was elected the state's first Republican governor in 1962 and often called upon Stewart for advice on human relations questions.

and picketing magnified the protest movement. The daily coverage of the demonstrations by Oklahoma City media reminded many whites that the problems of segregation could not be swept under a rug and forgotten."[18]

On July 2, 1964, President Johnson signed into law the Civil Rights Act of 1964, the most sweeping national statement condemning discrimination in public accommodations and employment since the days of Reconstruction following the Civil War.

The question of why the non-violent methods of the Oklahoma City NAACP succeeded in breaking down the walls of segregation in the late 1950s and early 1960s has been considered by many writers and historians.

There is a consensus among reviewers that, as Stewart predicted, the age of the protesters had a soothing effect upon whites who were less threatened by the youngsters than they might have been by black adults. Second, discipline of the protesters was a major factor in their success. From Stewart's directives, and from the day-to-day shepherding by Luper, the Oklahoma City Youth Council members conducted themselves above reproach, never retaliating even when spat upon, cursed at, and called the worst of tasteless racial names.

Oklahoma City police closely monitored the sit-ins and warned or arrested white hecklers. The sympathetic attitude of Governors Edmondson and Bellmon, and Oklahoma City Mayor Wilkes, made the path smoother on the road to final victory.

Author Jimmie Lewis Franklin's thought that talk, not violence, made a difference:

> The rhetoric of Black Power was more noticeable in Oklahoma than outright violent militancy. The NAACP, the Urban League, and groups such as Stewart's Oklahomans for Progress, never lost control of the civil rights movement in the state. They had much more rhetoric; they had the power, the influence, the resources, and the know-how. And importantly, they had a consciousness of history which had enabled them to fight continuously for many years.[19]

FIFTEEN
STILL MORE TO DO

STEWART never ran short of worthwhile projects to better living conditions in Oklahoma City. He had a full-time job managing the ONG eastside office, which was growing in importance and number of employees, because of new customers added as additional housing was constructed in the northeast area of the city. The company continued to support Stewart in his civic activities, giving him time off almost every day to work on projects or attend meetings.

Blacks celebrated the end of segregation in public accommodations, accomplished by nearly a decade of protest and negotiation. However, black Oklahomans still faced discrimination in employment and housing. The black population in Oklahoma City was concentrated on the northeast side, largely due to artificial barriers such as restrictive covenants and discrimination by lending institutions.

When Stewart's mentor, Roscoe Dunjee, died March 1, 1965, Stewart took an active role in planning his funeral service. More than 400 mourners jammed into the New Hope Baptist Church for Dunjee's funeral. People came on crutches, the blind had to be led, and the young and old listened and remembered as speaker after speaker extolled the virtues and accomplishments of the late editor.

Old warriors like Thurgood Marshall and Amos T. Hall sat with Stewart and Oklahoma Governor Henry Bellmon on the front row. Marshall, destined to become America's first black United States Supreme Justice later the same year, eulogized his friend: "I believe you're put on earth to do a job. Some people do theirs, some don't... Roscoe Dunjee gave us inspiration to get the job done. He didn't wait for somebody else. He didn't back down, even when his own people said he was wrong."[1]

Stewart was chosen to write a special tribute to Dunjee in *The Black Dispatch*. Stewart called Dunjee an "unselfish patriot" who did more for human relations than anyone Stewart had ever known or read about. Stewart praised Dunjee for his peculiar kind of faith:

> He could sit down in his study and read a portion of the United States Constitution or portions of state statutes and define its meaning or intent, according to his interpretation. If he believed his interpretation to be possible or just, hell nor high water could hinder him from pursuing a course to vindicate his position. Surprisingly enough, although learned constitutional lawyers differed with him on many occasions, most of Dunjee's idea and faith were decided in his favor by the top jurists and courts of the land.[2]

Stewart never minded when people called him "a disciple of Dunjee."

One of the most difficult assignments Stewart ever tackled was his address to the faculty at Douglass High School in August, 1963. He had the task of convincing teachers of the importance of a high school and college education, even though Stewart had himself dropped out of college.

Stewart said the time for depending on Douglass High School's gloried history, the time for pointing to the best band and drum corps, to state championship athletic teams, and to outstanding Douglass alumni had passed. He said, "This is a serious matter which the faculty and staff must grapple with to find a solution."[3]

Stewart told Douglass teachers they had failed to prepare students for the real world, "You are not training students to barter at the job marketplace in today's world. Yes, the fitted one-third struggle out, go to college and return to teach others, to teach. But what about the other two-thirds?"[4]

The auditorium was quiet as Stewart spoke firmly, but softly, "We have sit-ins, squat-ins, lay-ins, kneel-ins, boycotts, selective buying, freedom rides, and even pole-sitters clamoring for better opportunities for our youngsters, but there can never be a mass demonstration suitable to train a person to earn his daily bread. This duty and responsibility is yours."[5]

Teachers were lectured by Stewart about putting too much blame on past discrimination for the failure of Douglass students to succeed in the job market, "This may still be a major cause, but what we need today is a cure. Social and educational ills within your field require the same careful, dedicated diagnosis as would the internist or the psychiatrist seeking truth and remedy in the body and mind."[6]

Stewart recognized he was speaking bluntly, maybe even harshly, but he was doing so in good faith because he "had been through the mill of real life." He reported that his visits to dozens of personnel offices in Oklahoma City plants and factories over the years had revealed that Douglass students were not being prepared adequately for good jobs.

Stewart closed his hard-hitting address with an admonition, "Those farthest behind in a foot race must run just a bit harder, and with more dedication, if they really desire to finish among the leaders. What we at Douglass, and Negroes throughout America must resolve here and now is to stop placing all of our ills and misgivings on the past and racial discrimination, admit the differential which has heretofore existed, and disregard or rather overcome all handicaps while joining in concert for full steam ahead."[7]

Stewart never liked "slackers." In counseling black or white employees, he emphasized the importance of showing up for work on time and putting in a full day's work. He quickly corrected any employee who insisted he or she deserved special treatment because of color.

From 1963 to 1968 racial conflict reared its ugly head in many American cities. There were riots from Birmingham, Alabama, to

Chicago, Illinois; Los Angeles, California; and Harlem in New York City. At the beginning of the Freedom Summer in Mississippi in 1964, three white civil rights workers were murdered, touching off riots and demonstrations across the land. The 1965 race riot in the Watts Section of Los Angeles was the most destructive in history. Between 1965 and 1968 a half million blacks in 300 cities took part in riots. Fifty thousand were arrested, 8,000 were injured, and an estimated $100 million in property damage was inflicted.

Stewart, along with other members of the national NAACP Board of Directors, was concerned about the violence. At a 1964 meeting in New York City, Stewart, who often served as the "scribe" for meetings in which position papers were developed, listened to other board members in a lengthy discussion of how the NAACP could diffuse riots while continuing to fight for civil rights.

The NAACP developed a seven-point plan to do whatever possible to stop spreading riots "which are doing grave harm to our efforts to alleviate root problems in the ghetto." The seven points were:

(1) Appeal to the community personally by television, radio, and press in the name of the NAACP to avoid or refrain from any unlawful acts, or violent activity.

(2) Urge mothers and fathers to discipline children by keeping them from participating in any criminal activity such as looting, burning, sniping.

(3) Call on city, state and federal officials to take corrective steps immediately to solve long-standing problems.

(4) Organize teen-age patrols to help keep things cool for the remainder of summer, and to ask city, state or business people to help finance such patrols.

(5) Call on all churches, including storefronts, to assist in getting the message to ghetto residents that solutions to socio-economic problems cannot come through unlawful acts.

(6) Convene emergency steering committee of community leaders including representatives of police, news media, city government and hold daily meetings to check out rumors, issue cor-

rect information, and clear all such information through a responsible central source.

(7) Launch immediately a voter registration drive as a means of convincing public officials that we do not condone such mob violence, nor do we approve of their inaction which may have alleviated such strife. And last, but not least, appeal for NAACP memberships to strengthen the most responsible voice of the Negro community.[8]

Stewart returned to Oklahoma City and set out to accomplish the objectives commanded by the national NAACP board of directors. His efforts, and the efforts of other Oklahoma City black leaders who believed non-violent protest was the only successful means of dissent, were greatly responsible for Oklahoma City being spared from rioting, injuries, deaths, and property damage that plagued many cities in the United States in the 1960s.

Stewart's position with ONG gave him instant credibility and respect with many leaders of government and private industry. His counsel was sought when projects involved northeast Oklahoma City or the state's black population in general. His status with the company also afforded him substantial opportunity to get his message of equality into the hands of the most prestigious groups.

Stewart was invited to address a closed-door meeting of the leadership of the Oklahoma City Chamber of Commerce in July, 1967. His topic was the current problems besetting many of the nation's cities. Stewart told the chamber of the accomplishments of the NAACP but said blacks had done about all they could to accomplish equality, "From the national level of the NAACP, we believe conservative and/or constructive Negro leadership has done about all we are empowered to do toward a cure for this American illness without the aid, concern and assistance of you who are the cornerstone in our nation's economy." Stewart said the white business leaders must roll up their sleeves and work alongside black leaders to cure social ills.[9]

True to his reputation of "telling it like it is," Stewart lambasted businessmen for resting on their laurels as good citizens just because they had reached their annual quota in the United Fund and

Red Cross campaigns and by establishing a token policy of fair employment in their factories, plants, and stores.

Stewart said Oklahoma City's business community did not rank very high in the public opinion poll he conducted daily in the slums by talking with the poor, "It is not enough to only see the inner city from your office window, or catch snatches of it through the rear view mirror on your daily in and out expressway journey to and from suburbia."[10]

Stewart called upon the Chamber of Commerce to help solve a long list of socio-economic problems, including inadequate schools, poor or non-existent health care, job discrimination, poor housing, cultural barriers, police rudeness, lack of personal respect, loan sharking, unsound welfare programs, hostility, and hopelessness.[11]

Stewart frequently conferred with police chiefs in Oklahoma City and surrounding communities about a myriad of problems, including allegations of brutality and job discrimination. The few black policemen who were hired were rarely promoted and were segregated by being forced to patrol only the black areas of town.

In early 1965 Stewart approached Oklahoma City Police Chief Hilton Geer to request more jobs for blacks. Geer promised to look for good black applicants. However, when nothing happened to remedy the inequities perceived by the black community, Senator E. Melvin Porter, Clara Luper, and Linda Pogue, president of the NAACP Youth Council, led a march on the police station April 4, 1965. Part of the protest was against what Luper called police brutality in the beating the previous week of a woman who was arrested on a traffic complaint.

Stewart was invited to the White House August 6, 1965, for President Johnson's signing of the Voting Rights Act of 1965. Stewart and the NAACP national board had worked for years for federal legislation to overcome what he called the "crippling legacy of bigotry and injustice" in voting rights for blacks in the South. The 1965 legislation banned literacy requirements for voting. The direct and immediate result of the law was the registration of hundreds of thousands of new voters over a short period of three years.

In Mississippi alone, the numbers of black voters increased from 28,500 in 1964 to 251,000 in 1968. More black voters led to more black officials and caused white officials to be more sensitive to the needs of black constituents[12].

In June, 1966, Stewart attended a White House Conference on Civil Rights, the brainchild of President Johnson who called the conference to "find ways to combat the remaining obstacles to black participation in American life."[13]

At first, Dr. Martin Luther King, Jr. was not invited to the conference primarily because of his opposition to the Vietnam War. However, Stewart, Roy Wilkins, and other black leaders prevailed upon organizers of the conference to include King because of his tremendous influence on many black Americans involved in the civil rights struggle.

The conference debated education, housing, racial injustice, and welfare. Many of the recommendations that came out of the conference ultimately ended up as federal law in the Civil Rights Act of 1968.

A close association with Oklahoma United States Senator Fred Harris allowed Stewart to provide his input in a national study of conditions that fed the racial unrest in the mid-1960s. Harris was chosen by President Johnson in 1967 as a member of the National Advisory Commission on Civil Disorders, commonly known as the Kerner Commission because of its chairman, Illinois Governor Otto Kerner, Jr.; NAACP Executive Director Roy Wilkins; New York Mayor John Lindsay; Harris; United States Senator Edward W. Brooke of Massachusetts; and United Steelworkers President I. W. Abel joined five other prominent Americans as members of the Commission.

Harris asked Stewart to provide information and make recommendations concerning the study. Stewart met with Harris and presented his views of injustices and conditions in America's ghettoes that created tinderbox conditions. Harris was especially interested in how black leaders in Oklahoma had avoided the violence-filled conflict.

The Kerner Commission concluded the nation was moving toward two separate societies, one black, one white, separate and un-equal.[14] The report urged the federal government to design massive programs to seek and end to hunger, poverty, social disorganization, and ignorance.

Stewart was concerned about employment statistics which revealed that only 133 blacks held good-paying federal jobs among 44,000 federal government employees in the Oklahoma City area. Stewart expressed disappointment that blacks comprised only three and a half percent of the state government work force, most of them earning less than $3,000 per year.[15]

Stewart created a firestorm of controversy in 1966 when he accused the state's largest employer, Tinker Air Force Base, and the Federal Aviation Administration facility at Will Rogers World Airport, with employment discrimination.

From the Pentagon and the commander of Tinker came wholesale denials that blacks were not given equal opportunity for federal jobs. Officials at both Tinker and the FAA had complied with new federal laws in establishing equal employment opportunity guidelines. However, Stewart believed that the best-paying jobs were not being made available to blacks and other minorities.

Tinker commander Major General Melvin McNickle strongly denied that the personnel office at Tinker was biased against blacks. McNickle said his objective was to assure minority employees equal treatment in all facets of employment. The general also said he agreed with edicts from the United States Civil Service Commission that indicated that true equal opportunity exists only when the ratio of employment in each occupation, grade and organization is commensurate with that in the community.

Stewart was unhappy with the reality that blacks comprised 15 percent of Oklahoma City's population in 1965 but only eight percent of the work force at the sprawling Midwest City air base. More disappointing was the fact that blacks held mostly lower-paying jobs.

Stewart met with leaders of several black organizations to draft specific recommendations for General McNickle to utilize to improve opportunities for blacks at Tinker. Stewart enlisted the help of United States Senator Mike Monroney who took immediate action. Monroney called Civil Service Commission Chairman John Macy and complained bitterly that no blacks were employed in the Fair Employment Office at Tinker.

Monroney also took to heart Stewart's complaints that the personnel office at Tinker often devised unnecessary tests that effectively eliminated blacks from qualifying for certain positions. Monroney insisted that "some way be found to qualify a larger number of Negroes in Government installations, particularly in the big ones such as the FAA and Tinker, and to find ways of eliminating foolish and unnecessary examination requirements that do not necessarily pertain to the job being sought."[16]

Stewart used his soft-spoken presentation and diplomacy skills to convince General McNickle to revamp the Fair Employment Office at Tinker. Stewart monitored the employment situation at Tinker and happily reported a year later that dozens of qualified blacks had been hired or promoted under the new equal employment policy.

SIXTEEN
URBAN RENEWAL

HOUSING in some of the original areas of black settlement, just south and east of downtown Oklahoma City, was never adequate, but by the 1960s was despicable and basically uninhabitable. The word "slum" was a vivid and real description for many private residences and antiquated rooming houses.

Stewart's heart was heavy when he drove down streets he roamed as a child and saw old friends living in the worst possible housing, mere shacks on rotting foundations, some without indoor plumbing.

Stewart campaigned for 30 years for better housing for blacks in Oklahoma City but several hurdles stood in his way.

Homeowners and landlords lacked the capital necessary to improve and repair houses and commercial buildings in the area. Blacks were trapped. Even with changes in the legal landscape which allowed them to live basically anywhere they desired, the lack of money mired many blacks in sub-standard homes.

Another problem was the inaction of the federal and state government to remedy inadequate housing conditions.

In the final years of the administration of President Dwight D. Eisenhower, America renewed its effort to improve housing for poverty-stricken families who could not help themselves. Federal funds were appropriated to help states and cities plan the renewal of blighted urban areas. The program was appropriately dubbed "urban renewal."

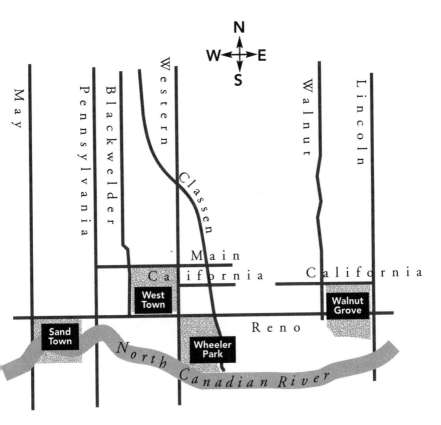

PROMINENT EARLY BLACK COMMUNITIES IN OKLAHOMA CITY

Oklahoma's legislature authorized urban renewal programs in 1959. On November 2, 1961, the Oklahoma City City Council created the city's first Urban Renewal Authority (URA). Original commissioners were Granville Tomerlin, chairman; F. D. Moon, vice chairman; C. Kenneth Woodard, secretary-treasurer; Reuben G. Martin and Joe C. Scott, members.[1]

The urban renewal program was, in concept, what Stewart had dreamed of as he saw his community decaying. He and his neighbors wanted good streets, clean alleys, and decent housing for the tens of thousands of blacks who did not want to leave the area of town where they had lived most of their lives. But the lack of resources had left the blighted areas without much hope.

The first urban renewal project approved by the City Council was the University Medical Center project in 1965. Stewart was appointed to the project's advisory committee with other black leaders Reverend Goree James; Dr. Frank Cox; Reverend Joe Edwards; Mrs. J. M. Littlepage; A. D. Mathues; Dr. E. C. Moon, Jr.; Bishop F. C. Scott; Earl Temple; and Reverend E. J. Perry.

Stewart was an avid supporter of early urban renewal efforts. He agreed with the URA's stated goals of renovating homes that were worthy of saving, clearing slums, and redeveloping vacant land left by the process.

The original University Medical Center project envisioned improving living conditions for 2,000 residents in a 240-acre tract bounded on the north by Northeast Thirteenth Street, the east generally by Stonewall Avenue, the south by Northeast Fourth Street, and the west by the right-of-way for the planned Capitol Expressway, ultimately built as the Centennial Expressway in the late 1980s.

Facing: Dilapidated
residential housing in
northeast Oklahoma City
alarmed City leaders who
pushed for urban renewal.
Right: The wrecking ball of
urban renewal destroys the
John A. Brown Department
Store in Oklahoma City.
Below: A house at 911
Northeast Fourth Street
became the two hundreth
structure to be removed in
the University Medical
Center urban renewal
project in 1967. (Photos
Courtesy *The Daily
Oklahoman*.)

The original project also
called for the construction of
three blocks of townhouse
apartments for low to medi-
um-income families, a six-
acre retail shopping center,
and the rehabilitation of 121
houses moved from cleared
areas to scattered sites throughout the renewal area.[2]

Rehabilitation was a key element of the University Medical
Center project. More than 3,000 buildings were slated for repair
to bring them up to Urban Renewal Authority standards. Federal
funds were provided for up to $1,500 grants for each individual
homeowner. Low-interest loans up to $10,000 were available.

Stewart spent hundreds of hours talking to URA board members and citizens affected by the project to solve problems caused by the massive project. In 1965, he was present at the home of Mrs. Emma Fullbright when she became the first homeowner relocated. Urban renewal allowed her to move from her ramshackle home on Northeast Ninth Street to a new home on Northeast Forty-fifth Street.

A year later, Beatrice Lewis' home in the 900 block of Northeast Eighth Street was the first home to be rehabilitated. Mrs. Lewis qualified for a $1,500 grant and a $600 three-percent loan.[3]

An even larger urban renewal project, the John F. Kennedy Project, was launched by the city council in May, 1966. The project encompassed a large blighted area from the Medical Center area east to Interstate 35, bounded on the north by Northeast Twenty-third Street and on the south by the MK&T Railroad tracks south of Northeast Fourth Street. It was the largest urban renewal project in area west of the Mississippi River.[4] The 1,257-acre project contained 18,000 people occupying 5,610 homes and 418 non-residential buildings.[5]

The URA came under heavy fire from Stewart and other black leaders shortly after the JFK Project was announced. Stewart's primary complaint was that URA officials were in so much hurry to secure government funding of the project that blacks were not consulted with, or kept informed, about what changes the massive project might bring to the black community.

Stewart charged that URA officials were resistant to his suggestion that the project also include a large area of sub-standard housing south of Northeast Fourth Street. Stewart criticized leadership decisions of James T. Yielding, executive director of the URA, who came to Oklahoma City from Cleveland, Ohio, where he oversaw that city's urban renewal program. Stewart's NAACP friends in Cleveland reported a ten-year battle with Yielding over urban renewal issues.

Citing a "general lack of communication," Stewart publicly questioned the propriety of the JFK Project in early June, 1966. Stewart appeared at a city council meeting wearing his official hat as president of the Citizens' Chamber of Commerce (formerly the Negro Chamber of Commerce), a post he held since the early 1960s. Stewart repeated questions he said he was hearing on the eastside, "Why pick on our side of town? When do we learn just when we have to move? Why not go south of Fourth Street where there's a real blighted area?"[6]

Stewart charged that citizens on the eastside had been misled and shown incorrect maps detailing the scope of the JFK Project. Stewart bitterly opposed URA plans to destroy some of the black community's best and largest homes between Northeast Eighth and Thirteenth streets and Stonewall and Lottie.

Stewart's biggest complaint was that the advisory committee of which he was a member had never been called together during the planning stage of the JFK Project.

Stewart challenged URA officials to publicly debate the merits of his complaints in a television program. Ernie Schultz of WKY-TV invited Stewart and URA director Yielding, or his assistant, Don Sullivan, to appear on a weekly public affairs show, "Point of View." When the URA officials fail to show up at the television station for taping the program, Stewart accused them of "chickening out."[7]

Stewart met with other black leaders who supported his position that urban renewal in Oklahoma City would not proceed unless blacks directly affected by the projects were consulted with. Stewart convinced Henry Floyd, president of the Oklahoma City NAACP Branch, and State Representative John B. White to stand with him in opposition to the proposed JFK Project.

Other black leaders such as State Senator E. Melvin Porter, Reverend Goree James, president of the Interdenominational Ministerial Alliance, and Dr. Charles Atkins openly supported the project, causing *The Daily Oklahoman* to conclude that "A power struggle among leaders of the city's Negro community was blamed by some for adding to the controversy."[8]

Stewart pleaded for black unity:

Dividing the Negro community like casting lots for the remains of a dead man is not the solution. This is what some forces in Oklahoma City would love. And mark my word, they are working at it day and night. Until that day comes when forces outside of the Negro community recognize us as people and are willing to work and plan WITH US rather than FOR US, the better road for all to travel is the straight and narrow path within the framework of established organizations who have kept the faith thus far. Together we stand, divided we fall.[9]

Stewart met privately with Mayor George Shirk who admitted that "some of the objections are well-taken."[10] The mayor agreed with Stewart that the URA had over-planned and may have been too ambitious in some ways. Shirk asked Stewart to sit down with URA officials and work out their differences.

Representative White and Stewart called for the resignation of URA director Yielding, primarily because of what they perceived as his inability to work with advisory committees from the areas affected by urban renewal.

The Daily Oklahoman wholeheartedly endorsed the entire JFK Project but agreed with Stewart that the area south of Northeast Fourth Street must be cleared. "This truly is a blighted area. . . Negroes well could ask why it was left untouched when better housing areas to the north and northeast were being chosen for renewal. Now that will be rectified."[11] The newspaper also echoed Stewart's complaint about communication: "It is reported that the urban renewal officials have not always been clear in what they said. Certainly the renewal agency constantly must evaluate itself to be sure it is being absolutely explicit and candid with all concerned."[12]

City officials spurned Stewart's attempts to put the JFK Project temporarily on hold. Stewart wrote in his weekly column in *The Black Dispatch*, "We lost the first round in our efforts to bring a worthwhile and meaningful urban renewal program to the east side of Oklahoma City. However, 'the darkest part of the night is just before the dawn,' and our numbers are legion who still have hope. Some of us will be living here, and most likely in homes of our choice, long after many of those false prophets have gone with the wind or back where they came from."[13]

Stewart was optimistic that black leaders could somehow convince URA officials to not tear down more than 100 of the finest homes owned by blacks in the city. Those homes were just south of University Hospital and the Medical Center area. Stewart wrote, "Oklahoma City has a golden opportunity presently to chase the money-changers out of the temple if we remain steadfast."[14]

Stewart took the lead in the black community to negotiate needed changes in the JFK Project. An all-night secret meeting of black leaders was held on June 10. During the meeting, which ended at 5:00 A.M., Stewart talked twice with URA assistant director Don Sullivan.

At a Sunday afternoon meeting of the NAACP local branch, 150 blacks debated whether or not to endorse the JFK Project. Finally, Stewart, the peace-maker, made a motion to endorse the entire urban renewal program in northeast Oklahoma City. A newspaper account of the meeting said "angry condemnation of urban renewal spiced the meeting but only six voted against the resolution."[15]

One of the fruits of Stewart's many years of service in Oklahoma City was his familiarity with almost everyone in power, in business and in government. His relationship with Ralph Bolen, a local automobile dealer who was chairman of the URA board of directors, may have saved the future of the entire urban renewal effort in Oklahoma City. Bolen suggested, and Stewart agreed, that the NAACP appoint a committee to negotiate differences with the URA board.

Negotiations resulted in several changes in the sprawling JFK Project. Stewart was not completely satisfied with the final plan, but noted the good aspects of the project far outweighed any less desirable consequence. In later years, Stewart and Reverend W. K. Jackson agreed that Oklahoma City's urban renewal projects were good for the community but charged that two critical mistakes were made. The area south of Northeast Fourth Street was never redeveloped and too many of the blacks' finest homes south of the Medical Center were needlessly destroyed.

In less than a decade, $200 million was spent on urban renewal projects in northeast Oklahoma City. Nearly 1,500 homes were remodeled and 130 new houses constructed. The Oklahoma City Housing Authority built a 200-unit Marie McGuire Plaza elderly housing project at Northeast Twelfth Street and Lottie. New streets were paved and sewer and water lines installed. A new fire station at Northeast Twenty-first Street and Eastern Avenue and a new city library at Northeast Twenty-third Street and Eastern Avenue were planned. A new city convention center, the Myriad, resulted from the urban renewal effort.

Stewart used the Citizens' Chamber of Commerce as a springboard for presenting critical issues to the City Council of Oklahoma City. In November, 1967, Stewart and Dr. A. L. Dowell prevailed upon the council for the umpteenth time to pass a fair housing ordinance, guaranteeing blacks the right to live and prosper in any neighborhood.

The Mayor's Community Relations Commission, of which Stewart was a member, proposed a far-reaching ordinance that would sweep into history any vestiges of segregation in housing in Oklahoma's capital city.

After much heated debate, the council defeated the proposed ordinance, prompting Dr. Dowell to begin a one-man stand-in demonstration. The eastside optometrist pledged to stand for the duration of all city council meetings until a fair housing ordinance was enacted into law. Dowell's stand-in lasted three months.

Stewart verbally lashed out at city leaders who would not support a fair housing law, "You have schemed and planned to put disadvantaged citizens, primarily Negroes, further in the ditch." [16]

While Stewart was verbally sparring with white leaders opposed to fair housing, Clara Luper led 350 demonstrators from the Freedom Center in northeast Oklahoma City to Hillcrest Shopping Center at Southwest Fifty-ninth Street and Pennsylvania Avenue. Over the next few days demonstrators also marched by the homes of city council members and Mayor James Norick to point out the need for open housing in the city.

City Councilman Ben Franklin introduced another open housing ordinance just before the end of 1967. The new proposal promised to secure for all people "equal access to housing in all neighborhoods," which was nothing but a restatement of recognized federal law.[17]

Stewart met with Councilman Franklin who emerged from the meeting with Stewart's promise that black leaders would accept the watered-down ordinance that contained less stringent penalties than the Citizens' Chamber of Commerce-backed ordinance.

Stewart urged his readers in *The Black Dispatch* to unite and back the proposed desegregation ordinance, "Every church in greater Oklahoma City should urge its membership to write, wire or give personal evidence of their belief in the brotherhood of man. Minorities, too, have a responsibility. Ours is not to prove ourselves, since we are all children of God, and all created in His image. However, we do have a responsibility and that is to try to seek a satisfactory solution 'with malice toward none and charity for all'."[18]

Finally, in July, 1969, the city council passed the ordinance making it illegal for anyone, including homeowners and real estate agents, to discriminate because of race, color, religion, or national origin. The law was officially on the books, but the reality of segregation would live on.

SEVENTEEN
SONIC BOOMS AND A
GARBAGE STRIKE

IN THE 1960S Stewart used the power of the press and his weekly column in *The Black Dispatch* to mold public opinion on a variety of issues. In expressing support for three state questions designed to streamline Oklahoma's road-building program and create a State Highway Commission, Stewart pointed to the accomplishments of Governor J. Howard Edmondson.

Stewart credited Edmondson with "fighting hard" to eliminate job and housing discrimination. Stewart lauded Edmondson for appointing leading black citizens to state positions. He mentioned the appointments of Emery Jennings of Muskogee to the Pardon and Parole Board; Ira Hall of Oklahoma City to the Commission of Higher Education; Wayne C. Chandler, Oklahoma City, as an inspector with the Alcoholic Beverage Control Board; Reverend C.C. Rhone, Oklahoma City, as a parole officer; A. C. Shoats, Muskogee, as an inspector with the State Highway Department; Eva M. Austin and Wilhelmina Fisher, Oklahoma City, as social workers; and Mrs. Melvin Porter as secretary of the State Human Relations Commission.[1]

In 1964, sonic booms, emanating from low-flying jets landing and taking off at Tinker Air Force Base, became a source of protest for many citizens. The City Council of Oklahoma City voted to ask the Air Force to end the tests because one landlord reported losing $80 per month in rental income.

Stewart chided the city council for overreacting, "If we want progress, more jobs and greater growth in Oklahoma City, someone must pay the cost. Nearly every step forward we've made within the past 40 years has met some opposition. Some didn't want Lake Hefner. Others thought we should keep the zoo down in the river bottoms on South Western, and brother, we could enumerate objections until the Fourth of July, but citizens of vision prevailed and our city went forward. This reminds us of laws and ordinances passed at the turn of the century against horseless carriages to protect the horses. Where are the horses now and is not our city a better and more progressive place in which to live?"[2]

Stewart was never hesitant to openly critique the actions of other black leaders who he saw as trying to promote individual popularity rather than further the common cause of equality. He said an effective civil rights leader should operate like a football quarterback, "First he doesn't give away his strategy to the opposition. If bucking the line gets no results, a thinking quarterback would try a forward pass or an end run. There are more ways to score than one."[3] Stewart ended one column with, "Yes, we're just as strong for civil rights and all the privileges of first class citizenship as ever, but bluffing and mouthing is not the solution to our problems."[4]

After the City Council of Oklahoma City again refused to pass an ordinance banning discrimination in public accommodations in March, 1964, E. Melvin Porter, president of the Oklahoma City NAACP branch, called for another general boycott of the downtown area.[5]

Stewart, as a member of the national board of the NAACP and president of the Citizens' Chamber of Commerce, adamantly opposed the boycott. He was a member of the Community Relations Commission and believed progress was being made in healing the division between the races. Stewart and Dr. Charles Atkins said a boycott was not in the best interest of the community as a whole, including the black community. Stewart expressed his view in "Jimmy Says": "Many of us are just as concerned with the welfare of this city and the elimination of every vestige of segregation as Mr. Porter is, but we are not going to attempt to stop an elephant with a fly swatter."[6]

With the help of United States Senator Mike Monroney, Stewart won the appointment of several blacks to civil service boards of a dozen federal government agencies in the Oklahoma City area in 1964. Stewart considered the appointments very important for the long-range success of a program to promote better-paying government jobs for blacks. Stewart gave much of the credit for the appointments to the Oklahoma City Area Employment Caucus, comprised of seven major civil rights organizations, that placed political pressure "where it would serve the best purpose for the greatest number."[7]

Jobs for citizens in the black community was an issue that traditionally was near the top of Stewart's list of priorities. He dug for statistics to prove his charge that blacks were discriminated against in employment. After a survey was made of federal government agencies in the mid-1960s, he wrote, "The report is too long to go into detail, but it didn't take a Philadelphia lawyer to see who, and to a large extent, why Ham's children were on the short end of the line."[8]

One of Stewart's dreams was realized when Dr. Charles Atkins became the first black member of the city council in Oklahoma City in September, 1966. Atkins and Stewart were usually on the same side of any particular issue and Stewart was elated at Atkins' appointment to fill the unexpired term of the late Councilman Guy James. Stewart wrote, "The City Council did more for our city's Negroes than we have done for ourselves. . . We have a Negro on this council. That is more than our combined efforts and votes could do in the last three city council elections."[9]

Frankly, Stewart thought about campaigning for his own appointment to replace Councilman James but decided against it, "We stayed as far away from the issue as a coon would a pack of braying hounds on a moonlit night."[10]

Stewart believed that Atkins, as a black man, could serve the northeast side of Oklahoma City better than "all of his predecessors put together. After all, he's just been colored 54 years, and brother, believe it or not, you learn something under those circumstances."[11]

"Jimmy Says" often congratulated blacks and whites for admirable accomplishments. When Mable Haywood retired in 1966 after 35 years as an employee of Oklahoma Natural Gas Company, Stewart applauded the efforts of his fellow employee, saying, "Before automation Mable took care of the flower fund and the mailing of condolences and earned the title of 'mother confessor' at ONG... which she watched grow from less than 100 employees to over 800 as she bids farewell."[12]

Stewart even used his column to promote his employer. Upon the celebration of the gas industry's 150th year in 1966, Stewart wrote, "Just a reminder that whether you know it or not, there's nothing like cooking with gas." [13]

Not many of the activities of Stewart's family escaped his attention in "Jimmy Says." In 1966, Jimmy, Jr. was serving in the United States Marine Corps in Vietnam. He sent his parents a postcard advertising the Tan-Loe Hotel in Saigon as having perfect security and fresh air. Stewart advised Jimmy, Jr. to "Take 'em up on as much of this jive as your dough will stand son. It sounds much better, plus far safer, than sleeping in two feet of water in a fox hole or having to wait until some of those guys shoot at you before you recognize whether they are friend or foe. Keep your powder dry."[14]

Stewart never lost his sense of humor in the decades of filling his column with news of his travels. While attending the 57th annual convention of the NAACP in Los Angeles in July, 1966, Stewart wrote, "The Fourth of July picnic at Pasadena's Brookside Park was well attended and believe you me, the food was delicious. Ran into Roy Moore and daughter of Oklahoma City, visiting his sister. I think Roy would agree, the most exciting thing at the picnic was a delegate from Washington, D.C. wearing a white bikini outfit which mother would have never approved."[15]

Stewart and other black leaders ran headlong into a major confrontation with Oklahoma City City Manager Robert Oldland in 1969 over pay and promotions for blacks employed in the city's sanitation department.

Eighty-five percent of the department's employees were black,

Below: Reverend W. K. Jackson reads his Bible in an Oklahoma City patrol wagon awaiting transport to the city jail. Jackson and other protesters were arrested for blocking sanitation trucks manned by replacement drivers during the sanitation workers' strike in 1969. (Courtesy *The Daily Oklahoman.*)

Facing top: Clara Luper, foreground, awaits the arrival of sanitation trucks during the 1969 sanitation workers' strike. At far right in dark suit is State Representative John B. White. (Courtesy *The Daily Oklahoman*.)

Below: Clara Luper, center, leads a protest march in downtown Oklahoma City in August, 1969 to show support for striking sanitation workers. From left to right, Detective Charles Hill (now a Special District Judge in Oklahoma County), Reverend Ralph Abernathy, head of the Southern Christian Leadership Conference, Luper, Reverend W. K. Jackson, and Dr. A. L. Dowell, later the leading figure in school desegregation. (Courtesy *The Daily Oklahoman*.)

but no blacks filled high administrative positions. Oldland and Clara Luper were 180 degrees apart on every issue in the controversy. Luper said Oldland was "a coward" and lacked the courage to debate. Oldland said Luper "cannot speak for the sanitation workers."16

Reverend W.K. Jackson formed the Coalition for Civic Leadership (CCL) to support Luper's call for a strike by sanitation workers. An emergency meeting in early August, 1969, between Oldland and Jackson, Luper, and other black leaders failed to diffuse the situation. Tensions mounted as Luper and Oldland glared at each other and called each other names. Oldland shouted, "Any worker that walks off the job is dismissed automatically and I'll replace those who refuse to work. There will be no strike."17

Sanitation workers walked off their jobs on August 19. Luper and others were arrested when they refused to move out of the way of garbage trucks manned by replacement white drivers as they departed the sanitation department's Westwood yard.

The entire black community rallied behind the workers. Well-attended rallies held at various churches reflected the determination of black citizens. The first rally was at the Greater Cleaves Memorial CME Church. A standing-room-only crowd heard Senator E. Melvin Porter say, "We've got to stick together. White people are smiling in our faces and stabbing us in the back. It's time that we tell these white folks like it is. Our garbage men are the backbones of this city."18

Bus loads and car loads of people rushed to the Westwood yard every morning at 5:30 A.M. to throw up a human barricade in front of the sanitation trucks. Every day more people were arrested, including NAACP national Youth Director James Brown, Jr. and Richard Dockery, NAACP regional director.

Even though her bond was paid, Luper refused to leave the jail for days, drawing national attention to the plight of the Oklahoma City sanitation workers.

Reverend Jackson's St. John's Missionary Baptist Church became the headquarters for sanitation workers and their families. Jackson had been a vocal force in the black community since the early 1950s and built the CCL into a powerful organization that impacted many issues concerning the black community. Jackson, as CCL chairman, and State Representative Archibald Hill, Jr., as vice chairman, mobilized black ministers and leaders to raise thousands of dollars to keep sanitation workers alive while closed-door meetings between Stewart, Councilman A. L. Dowell, and others attempted to end the impasse.

August, 1969, was hot and steamy in Oklahoma City. Nightly rallies at St. John's Missionary Baptist Church helped kindle the enthusiasm for the sanitation strike.

On August 19, dubbed later by Luper as "Black Friday," hundreds of protesters marched on the Westwood garage. Hundreds of city police officers and state troopers lined the streets, armed with riot sticks, tear gas, and shotguns. Four of the march's leaders, Dr. Dowell, Archibald, Hill, Roland Betts, and William Woodward were arrested and charged under a 1920 law for inciting a riot. The march paralyzed businesses and schools and concentrated media attention on the situation.

Reverend Ralph David Abernathy, Martin Luther King's successor as head of the Southern Christian Leadership Conference, led a march through downtown Oklahoma City on August 24

Stewart quietly negotiated with city officials to end the 1969 sanitation workers' strike.

and spoke to a thousand people inside and outside of St. John's Church that night. Abernathy preached long and hard, "I've come here to tell that city manager Pharaoh to let the sanitation workers go free, to tell Mayor Pharaoh to let my people go!"[19]

City Manager Oldland refused to meet with Abernathy, Reverend Jackson, and Luper. That action prompted protesters to march to Oldland's home on Ski Island Lake in northwest Oklahoma City. Hand in hand, demonstrators sang "We Shall Overcome." Reverend Jackson left his calling card in Oldland's front door.[20]

More arrests followed, including State Representative Hannah Atkins and Councilman Dowell. Meanwhile, Stewart helped Reverend Jackson raise money for the striking workers and talked to every member of the city council, urging them to pressure Oldland to move from his rigid stance.

Oklahoma Governor Dewey Bartlett called upon both sides to get together and talk. Eventually, Oklahoma City Chamber of Commerce Executive Director Paul Strasbaugh, civic leader Stanton L. Young, and other business leaders were appointed to a committee to meet with Reverend Jackson and his followers to work out details of a settlement that spared the city much bloodshed that resulted from similar protests in other parts of the nation. City fathers made good on their promises and raised salaries for sanitation workers and promoted deserving black employees into administrative positions. As Luper would have said, "Another wall had fallen."

EIGHTEEN
RESEGREGATION

RESEGREGATION did not become a word in the English language until after the evils of segregation were outlawed by the highest court in the land and after social forces insisting on division by race sneaked their way back into many of the nation's public schools.

In Oklahoma City, a decade after *Brown v. Board of Education of Topeka, Kansas,* public schools remained segregated. The board of education approved all the correct resolutions and made appropriate provision for allowing students to go to any school in a reasonable relationship to where the student lived. However, where the student lived was the problem.

A high percentage of black families lived in the near northeast quadrant of the city. Whites lived elsewhere. Therefore neighborhood schools, serving the residential areas around them, were segregated.

For several years after *Brown,* Stewart attended hundreds of meetings with other black leaders and school officials with one goal in mind. . . complete integration of Oklahoma City's public schools. Most historians who have written about the period credit Stewart with being a "major factor" in the ultimate desegregation of the city's schools.[1] Other black leaders who continued to work for complete integration were Roscoe Dunjee; Dr. H. W. Williamston, longtime state president of the NAACP; Reverend W. K. Jackson; attorney Henry Floyd; attorney Archibald Hill; educator F. D. Moon; Dr. A. L. Dowell; Vivian Dowell; attorney

John E. Green; and Clara Luper. Of course, there were many others who spent time and money to see that the fight did not wane.

The hope for true integration of the city's public schools was dashed by the board of education's transfer policy which allowed a loophole for educators to keep blacks in black schools and whites in white schools. As blacks moved into the east-central area of Oklahoma City, whites were allowed to transfer their children to mostly-white schools. Integration was not working.

In 1959, Dr. A. L. Dowell moved outside the Oklahoma City School District and enrolled his son, Robert, in the Pleasant Hill School District. But when Robert was old enough to enter high school in 1960, he was enrolled in the nearest school, all-black Douglass High School.

In 1961, Dr. Dowell requested his son be transferred to all-white Northeast High School. After a few battles with school officials, Robert's transfer to Northeast was approved. However, the school board made it so difficult for Robert to enroll, Dr. Dowell decided federal court action was the only answer.[2]

Stewart met with Dr. Dowell and his attorneys, John E. Green and U. Simpson Tate. Green later served for decades as first assistant United States Attorney for the Western District of Oklahoma. His service to his profession was outstanding. Tate was regional counsel for the NAACP for years. He practiced law in Wewoka, Oklahoma, and had his hand in most civil rights lawsuits for 25 years in the middle of the century.

In October, 1961, Dr. Dowell filed the lawsuit on behalf of his son. The legal goal of the suit was basic, to permanently enjoin the board of education from using any rules and regulations to maintain a segregated school system and to require the board to submit an official desegregation plan.

The Dowell case was assigned to United States District Judge Luther L. Bohanon, an Arkansas native who grew up as the son of a tenant farmer near Kinta in eastern Oklahoma. Bohanon worked his way through college and the law school at the University of Oklahoma where he graduated in 1927. He practiced law with classmate Alfred P. "Fish" Murrah in Seminole, Oklahoma, before moving to Oklahoma City. In 1961 Bohanon was appointed by President John F. Kennedy to the federal bench.

Bohanon took his assignment to the Dowell case seriously. For months he pored over stacks of charts, graphs, maps, and "future plans" of the board of education. Bohanon found staggering proof that public schools in Oklahoma City remained segregated. It had been seven years since *Brown* but there remained seven all-white high schools and one all-black high school, Douglass. The 169 white students who lived near Douglass were given transfers. The number of all-white and all-black elementary and junior high schools saw little change during the same period.[3]

In March, 1963, Bohanon handed down a thundering decision that found the Oklahoma City Board of Education guilty of enforcing a discriminatory student transfer policy that perpetuated segregation and of failing to have a sufficient plan for racial integration.[4]

For four years, the Dowell case was on appeal. In 1967, Oklahoma City School Superintendent Dr. Bill Lillard and the board of education were ordered to present Bohanon a specific plan for implementing a detailed desegregation plan prepared by a three-man panel nominated by Dr. Dowell and his attorneys. Stewart spent hundreds of hours analyzing boundary lines, school census sheets, and population information to assist Dowell's attorneys to present a workable plan.

More legal wrangling followed. Judge Bohanon ultimately imposed boundaries that forced the board of education to utilize bussing of students across town to formerly all-white or all-black schools to achieve racial integration in classrooms.

Bohanon never specifically ordered busing of students. However, the federal judge commented, "Busing of children to attend the public schools is neither new or novel. Thousands of students are bused daily in the District and as a matter of fact, throughout the state."[5]

The very word "busing" caused instantaneous problems between blacks and whites in Oklahoma City. When white leaders cried foul, Stewart wrote in his weekly column, "We are rather amused at so many citizens screaming to the high heavens about forced busing... but none of these voices were heard when little Black children were being bused all over creation... To Presiding Judge Luther Bohanon, we say: 'Ride on Brother, ride on.' " 6

The 1970 Oklahoma legislature passed House Bill 1517, a strong anti-busing law. Stewart sent a telegram to Governor Dewey Bartlett, urging the chief executive to veto the bill:

> As president of Oklahomans for Progress, we strongly urge you to use the power of your office to veto the most horrendous, repressive piece of legislation [passed this year]... This politically unethical legislation will do absolutely nothing toward achieving quality integrated education for our state, nor shall it alter or influence any future federal court decisions. It does indicate to what depths some lawmakers in our state will stoop to, thru bigoted repressive legislation, to kindle the fires of racism and misunderstanding at a time of crisis.7

Despite Stewart's pleas, Governor Bartlett signed the law. However, Judge Bohanon totally ignored the state legislative action.

President Richard Nixon told a nationwide television audience in March, 1972, that he was opposed to forced busing to achieve racial balance, and called upon Congress to overrule lower court decisions that had ordered busing. Nixon said the lower federal courts had "gone too far."8

The presidential declaration caused Stewart great concern. A regional NAACP training conference was scheduled the following week in Little Rock, Arkansas. Stewart lobbied the 350 delegates to the conference to adopt a sweeping resolution ratifying the group's "unflinching support of busing as a legitimate tool to achieve meaningful integration of our schools."9 The resolution severely criticized Nixon for his anti-busing stand, "You have threatened to shackle the courts and rewrite the Constitution... You have refused to consult with the recognized leaders of Black Americans... You have ignored the findings of every major study concerning the impact of racial segregation. . . You have used the high office of the Presidency to encourage a national mood of reacting and oppression by emotional appeals and obvious deceit."[10]

The busing controversy split the community. Demonstrations and counter-demonstrations marred the peaceful landscape of the capital city. On the first day of bussing in August, 1972, 3,500 busing opponents rallied at the state fairgrounds. Fights broke out at several schools. One student was killed.

White flight occurred on an unprecedented scale. Private schools sprang up overnight, an obvious attempt to keep white children from being bussed.

Two previously all-black schools, Dunjee Junior-Senior High School and Moon Junior High were closed. Nearly two-thirds of the students in the city school system changed buildings from 1971 to 1972. Stewart spent weeks before the beginning of the school term answering phone calls on the logistics of change and trying to dispel rumors. He and others met almost daily with school officials to smooth over rough spots that fueled tempers of both blacks and whites.

Oklahoma City's school population plummeted from 75,000 students in 1967 to a low of 36,500 in 1991, 24 years later. By 1997, the population had slowly moved upward to just under 40,000. However, only 14,563, or 36 percent of the students were white, the lowest number since busing began. That compares with nearly 50,000, or 72 percent white students in the system in 1971.[11]

The final verdict on the success or failure of integration of Oklahoma City's public schools may not come for decades. In 1997, 12 years after returning to a neighborhood school plan, 206 of the 209 students at Garden Oaks Elementary School were black. At the Martin Luther King, Jr. Elementary School, only six white students were in the student body of 303. Enrollment in Moon Middle School was 90 percent black, up from 53 percent the year before.[12] School board officials announced a high school redistricting plan was under consideration.[13]

NINETEEN
NO SLOWING DOWN

BY 1970 Stewart was almost 60 years old. However, he was in good health and the passion to help others enjoy a better life still burned brightly within his heart.

Stewart looked beyond the concepts of the civil rights movement, he was interested in the individuals whose lives were affected. His chest swelled with pride when Governor Dewey Bartlett appointed Tulsa native Charles L. Owens in 1968 as Oklahoma's first black district judge. During the Bartlett administration, Stewart helped Ronnie Johnson become the first black state trooper. He recommended his friend Wayne C. Chandler to serve in a number of high state government positions. Chandler headed the state's economic opportunity programs at the Department of Economic and Community Affairs and ultimately became Director of the Board of Affairs.

Stewart's life was full. He was a good husband and faithful Christian. He and Mae Lois enjoyed playing bridge, and entertaining friends, and working in their local church. Stewart played lots of golf and hardly ever missed Langston University and University of Oklahoma football games. Stewart enjoyed his two sons and daughter, his eight grandchildren, and one great-granddaughter.

Stewart continued his service on the national board of directors of the NAACP, and its executive committee, which required at least a quarterly trip to New York City. More than once, nosy baggage inspectors questioned sweet-smelling packages in Stewart's luggage. The smell emanated from tin-foil-wrapped Oklahoma

City barbecue, from Pulliam's. Stewart frequently carried ribs and pork to his childhood playmate Ralph Ellison who was a professor at New York University.

Stewart was one of the few links for Ellison to his early roots on Second Street in Oklahoma City. The two men often reminisced into the early morning hours. Ellison only returned to his home state a few times in the last half of his life. He said, "To go back and find that old Second Street environment gone is traumatic, it's sort of disturbing and I don't want to lose the memories. I don't want to lose my sense of how it was, because after all, that's where I came from."[1]

Although he never thought of himself as much of a golfer, even though he carried a handicap of 18, Stewart served on the Oklahoma City Golf Commission, and on the governing boards of the Salvation Army, State Fair of Oklahoma, United Way of Oklahoma City, YMCA, Langston University Alumni Association, University of Oklahoma Foundation, Oklahoma City Urban Renewal Authority, and the Urban League of Greater Oklahoma City.

Stewart was the veteran board member of the Urban Renewal Authority. His wisdom and clear understanding of issues impressed URA attorney Jerry Salyer. Over lunch or driving around town, Stewart told Salyer, later a judge of the Oklahoma Workers' Compensation Court, about suffering discrimination as a youngster and promising himself to make a difference for his people. Salyer fondly described Stewart as a man of "reason, fairness, and judgement."[2]

Stewart also served as a civil rights consultant to the Oklahoma City Police Department and often was contacted by businesses, large and small, who wanted to develop fair employment and antidiscrimination programs. He was president of Villa Savoy Inc., a 132-unit housing development at Northeast Twenty-third Street and Grand Boulevard. Dr. Byron Biscoe was vice president and Reverend Joe E. Edwards was secretary-treasurer of the housing project that obtained the first 221-D3 government-backed loan in the state. Villa Savoy was a forerunner of public housing projects eventually funded in great numbers across the country by the federal government. A brochure advertised Villa Savoy apartments as "the most for your rent dollar... with beautiful Westinghouse refrigerators... Venetian blinds... and ultra-modern Blue Star gas ranges and water heaters." [3]

Stewart was a member of the Capitol Medical Center Historical Preservation Commission. He also served as president of the Oklahoma City Community Action Agency, the local federally funded entity charged with carrying on the war against poverty. He also was president of the Langston–Douglass Athletic Association and was a board member of the Council for Resocialization of Ex-Offenders (CREO) and the Coalition of Civic Leadership. He was appointed to the Southern Regional Council board, the Episcopal Diocese of Oklahoma Committee on Church and Race, and the Oklahoma City Charter Revision Committee.

Stewart's service to the community was not without controversy. When he was removed from the Oklahoma City Community Relations Commission (CRC) in 1971, Stewart appeared before the city council and said he would not permit "recalcitrants in private life or governmental affairs" to silence him. Stewart called his dismissal from the CRC "the most disappointing development that I have encountered in better than a quarter century of volunteer service to my city."

The city council was unaware that new CRC Chairman Charles True, whom Stewart had never met, had decided Stewart's presence on the CRC was no longer needed. Councilwoman Patience Latting said Stewart's absence on the commission would be "a detriment" to the work of the commission[4].

Stewart's active life gave him plenty of opportunity to be involved in so many community affairs that he was never short of material for his weekly column in *The Black Dispatch*. He ballyhooed fund-raising drives, NAACP membership campaigns, and made note of old-timers visiting the area.

In 1971 when Oklahoma Third District Congressman Carl Albert was elevated to the position of Speaker of the United States House of Representatives, Stewart wrote that "all Oklahomans should take pride... We in the area of human relations maintain a warm spot in our hearts and memories... We respect him because of his ability, but developed a love for him because of his integrity... We have lived long enough to see Albert put to the test numerous times and he hasn't come up wanting. His is an idea whose fullness of time is at hand, and though belated, we are the benefactors as well as all mankind."[5]

Stewart used his column to pay tribute to Associate District Judge Amos T. Hall of Tulsa when Hall died in late 1971. Stewart said, "He was a rare breed. He walked the lonely road of the market place with the ease and dignity of a swan on a clear lake, yet he mingled with, counseled with and sat with potentates and chancellors as a gentleman, friend, and confident."

Hall, who represented Ada Lois Sipuel Fisher, and dozens of other clients in major civil rights cases, was honored by Stewart for being a lawyer who was on call 24 hours a day, seven days a week, "wherever needed to defend the rights and protect the privileges of his people." Stewart said he wondered how Hall ever earned a living as a lawyer because of his pro bono representation of hundreds of indigent men and women.[6]

In 1972 Stewart and several fellow members of the NAACP national board met in Washington, D.C., to lobby members of Congress who were putting the finishing touches on a sweeping piece of legislation to punish employers who discriminated against minority workers. Stewart was invited to the White House on March 8 when President Nixon signed the Equal Employment Opportunity Act into law.

When fire-bombings and shootings erupted in northeast Oklahoma City in June, 1973, Stewart pleaded for calm. A half-million dollars in property damage was overshadowed by one shooting death and four injuries in the melee. The C.R. Anthony store on Northeast Twenty-third Street was destroyed. Northeast High School was fire-bombed. Stewart asked the City Council of Oklahoma City to investigate the fire-bombings and offer a reward for the apprehension of those responsible. Stewart was worried that other businesses would move from northeast Oklahoma City if the violence continued.

The Oklahoma City Downtown Sertoma Club gave Stewart its prestigious "Service to Mankind Award" in 1975. Mayor Patience Latting presented Stewart the award and remarked that Stewart's long-standing devotion to the community was often in the background. Stewart was cited for achieving equal rights for everyone "in a peaceful manner."[7]

Stewart's job duties with Oklahoma Natural Gas changed in January, 1976. He was appointed assistant to William Nash "Bill" Pirtle, then the company's district vice president. Stewart's new job allowed him to concentrate more on community relations than on day-to-day management responsibilities of the northeast Oklahoma City office which was closed. ONG officials determined the office which Stewart had managed for more than three decades was no longer needed inasmuch as most gas customers paid their monthly bills by mail and service assignments were handled through the downtown ONG office.

The Service to Mankind Award of the Sertoma Club of Oklahoma City is presented to Stewart by Oklahoma City Mayor Patience Latting in 1975.

Pirtle and Stewart became close friends. Pirtle considered Stewart to be his mentor in race relations. Pirtle grew up in west Texas and had little exposure to blacks. He readily accepted Stewart's coaching on how to handle black employees and maintain good relations with the black community.

Stewart was an exemplary employee. He was always on time as the workday began, even though he often attended community meetings every night of the week. Stewart was sensitive to the feelings of his ONG supervisors. He had a sixth sense that allowed him to know when he was about to cross the line between good and bad company policy.

Stewart had a special way of presenting a request to Pirtle. Rather than stating simply his wants and desires, Stewart would arrive at Pirtle's office and begin a "parable" that led to a formal request. He often began his speech with, "Now, a couple of old Texans like us need to be together on this deal."

Stewart played a meaningful role in formulating ONG policy as it related to energy costs for poor customers. Pirtle encouraged Stewart to suggest programs that would benefit lower income families. Stewart provided input for the "Share the Warmth" plan, implemented by the company to allow customers to add a contribution to their monthly bills to help their less fortunate neighbors who had difficulty paying their gas bill.

Pirtle, who played a major role in the private sector's recommendations for reorganization of state government during the administration of Oklahoma Governor David L. Boren, said Stewart gave credibility to ONG in the black community. His presence helped make federal government audits of the company's affirmative action program smoother. More than once Stewart defused criticism of ONG by a disgruntled minority employee. Stewart was satisfied that the company was making a good faith effort to offer equal employment opportunities to employees of every color.

Stewart's own credibility was buoyed by the unfailing support shown him by ONG. In later years it was not unusual for Stewart to get a tear in his eye when he talked about how ONG had stood by him even in the toughest of times.[8]

In accepting his new job, Stewart paid tribute to the company that had been so good to him for almost 40 years, "Oklahoma Natural has given me quite a bit of latitude to work in the community and help people wherever we could. My company has made me look good as a civil rights leader. As I have preached for fair employment laws, ONG has bent over backwards trying to carry out an affirmative action program as an equal employment employer."[9]

ONG senior vice president Max L. Knotts wanted Stewart to spend more time working on the utility company's affirmative action program and to assist ONG customers who wanted help with their own affirmative action plans.

In 1976 Stewart won the Golden Plate Award, one of the highest awards of the NAACP. He was cited for his pioneer work in civil rights and for serving three terms as chairman of Region Six of the NAACP.

Stewart was interested in preserving black history. As early as 1968 he began promoting the writing of a history of blacks in Oklahoma, a history based on facts, not emotionalism or sentimentality. Stewart worked with Assistant Oklahoma City School Superintendent Dr. Mervel Lunn to draft Kaye M. Teall, a former teacher in the Norman Public School District, to compile what became the leading resource book of black history in Oklahoma. State and federal funds enabled the publication in 1971 of *Black History in Oklahoma—A Resource Book*. In the preface to the book, Teall wrote, "The full story needs to be told so that both black and white Oklahomans may have a better, more viable understanding of the past and of this morning's headlines."

Stewart served on the Editorial Advisory Committee for Teall's resource book. Other members of the advisory committee were Ada Lois Sipuel Fisher, Ruby W. Ewing, Eddie Jackson, F. D. Moon, and Vern Moore.

Stewart decided to retire from his full-time job at ONG on his 65th birthday in September, 1977. His bosses and ONG and state and local leaders planned a giant celebration and roast to commemorate his retirement and birthday.

Oklahoma United States Senator Henry Bellmon served as honorary chairman of the banquet at the Skirvin Hotel on September 16. It was a lavish affair with "roast beef, string beans almondine, rissolee potatoes, and walnut cake." The list of program participants, put together by *Black Dispatch* general manager Russell Perry, read like a "Who's Who in Oklahoma." The masters of ceremony were Oklahoma City University President Dr. Dolphus Whitten and former Langston University President Dr. Thomas English.

Roasters were E. M. "Jim" Lookabaugh from the Urban Renewal Authority; *Black Dispatch* publisher Dr. G. E. Finley; Reverend W. K. Jackson; Sig Harpman of the Oklahoma City Golf Commission; Margaret Bush Wilson, chairman of the national board of the NAACP; Dr. Helen Carter, chairman of the Humanities Department of Oscar Rose Junior College; Acting United States Attorney John E. Green; Oklahoma City Chamber of Commerce Manager Paul Strasbaugh; State Senator E. Melvin Porter; Stan McGehee; Eugene D. Jones, Jr.; State Representative Visanio

ONG official R.B. Nelson and Stewart announce a $1,000 donation in 1975 to the Ralph Ellison Library to help preserve black history.

Johnson; Wayne C. Chandler; Oklahoma Natural Gas Board chairman Charles C. Ingram; State Representative Hannah D. Atkins; Congressman Mickey Edwards; Assistant Fire Chief Carl Holmes; and Senator Henry Bellmon.

ONG Chairman Ingram called Stewart "a rare individual who faithfully serves his employer, his community, and his people." Ingram was proud of Stewart's service to ONG, the giant utility that Ingram joined in 1940 and rose to the position of chairman of the board in 1966.[10]

Senator Bellmon said Stewart had provided stability in the black community and had bettered the lives of all Oklahomans. He continued, "Indeed the entire state owes him a real debt of gratitude." Bellmon believed Stewart's modest start with ONG as a janitor possibly was the key to his success, "Maybe that's why Stewart feels perfectly at home giving aid to the most impoverished one day, and giving advice to the governor the next. He's comfortable dealing with people from all walks of life, and perhaps that's the reason he has a tendency to be heard."[11]

Seven hundred friends and admirers heard Stanton L. Young brag on Stewart for his service as a "human bridge between Oklahoma City's black and white communities, walking with those in power but marching with those who were powerless."[12]

Dr. Whitten lightened up the occasion by using a cowbell to make certain that all of Stewart's roasters did not exceed their three-minute time limitation.

After all the roasting and toasting, an overwhelmed Stewart took the podium and was greeted by a standing ovation. He said his civic work was never done for praise but that "it just seemed to be the right thing to do." With tears in his eyes, Stewart told the admiring throng, "As a youngster, I used to walk these streets past this hotel. I never dreamed I would be honored in it one day. In those days, we weren't even allowed in such places."

Stewart added as an afterthought, "But don't forget, we still have a job to do."[13]

Stewart gave his collection of books, correspondence, documents, and newspaper clippings to the Ralph Ellison Library for safekeeping. ONG granted sufficient money to the library to catalogue and shelve the collection. The *Oklahoma City Times* called the collection "one man's chronicle of the civil rights movement he helped to shape."

In a feature article in the *Times,* Stewart was called "the scrappy black man who never tried to be popular."Reporter Warren Vieth said, "His searing comments about the plight of Oklahoma City blacks have punctuated scores of city council meetings. His eloquent opposition to capital punishment's racial overtones has reverberated through the halls of the state capitol. . . For many years he was a thorn in the sides of white officials who thought Stewart's people should stay on their traditional side of the tracks."[14]

In the newspaper story, Stewart recalled when he was approached by a rich white woman during the height of street demonstrations in downtown Oklahoma City. The woman asked, "Stewart, isn't it a shame that these kids are out on the street marching and carrying on?" Stewart replied, "No ma'am, I think it's a shame that they have to get out on the street, and march just to get a hamburger or a bottle of pop at the store."

Stewart told the newspaper that even though he was retiring from full-time employment, someone had to continue the struggle for civil rights, "Civil rights disrupts everything. Maybe you would rather be watching the TV or playing golf, but it calls you elsewhere. It is still calling me."[15]

TWENTY
AN ACTIVE RETIREMENT

AFTER RETIREMENT some men are content to sit on the front porch and gaze at passing cars all day. Others try to convince their wives they love fishing six days a week. Not Jimmy Stewart.

Stewart continued his long association with Oklahoma Natural Gas Company as a consultant. Energy was on the minds of many Americans in 1977. An energy shortage brought about the need for a national energy policy.

Working for Oklahoma's largest natural gas company, Stewart was recognized as a spokesman for the energy industry. Stewart did not necessarily know the technical and scientific side of the gas business, but always called upon fellow ONG employees to provide statistical and technical data for his presentations. He was sought out by colleges and universities and chambers of commerce who needed energy company representatives to address students and energy conferences.

The NAACP held a national conference on the energy crisis in Washington, D.C., in mid-November, 1977. The organization established a special committee on energy and named Stewart chairman. His assignment was to develop position papers and action programs to protect the rights of poor people from inflationary trends and potentially devastating impact of energy price increases.

The Washington, D.C., meeting was seen by NAACP Executive Director Benjamin L. Hooks as a major undertaking in an uncharted area for a civil rights organization. Frankly Stewart had urged the NAACP to take a position on energy because many impoverished Americans spent a large percentage of their disposable income on energy. Stewart considered the potential harm from high energy costs as destructive as high housing and food costs for blacks throughout the nation. Secretary of Energy James Schlesinger addressed the NAACP Energy Committee at the Mayflower Hotel urging Stewart and the 17 other committee members to closely study President Stewart Carter's proposed national energy policy.

For the following seven weeks Stewart worked day and night to write an energy policy that was good for both poor Americans and for public utilities and private companies that supplied the energy.

Below: When Stewart retired he contributed his papers to the Ralph Ellison Library. Metropolitan Library director Lee Brawner and Stewart admire a bulletin board outlining the scope of the papers called the Black Heritage Chronicles. (Courtesy *The Daily Oklahoman.*)

Above: Stewart was awarded the NAACP's Golden Plate Award in 1976.

He consulted with officials of ONG and other utilities and read stacks of documents regarding oil and gas production.

In January, 1978, Stewart presented the NAACP *Energy Statement* for approval of the national board of directors. The Statement criticized President Jimmy Carter's plans to severely limit domestic production of oil and gas. Stewart's central idea was to encourage the development of all forms of energy—solar, geothermal, biomass, tidal, oil shale, and synthetic fuels from coal, as well as nuclear. The *Statement* said the key to future needs was a suitable energy mix that would afford an adequate supply of energy.

NAACP Board Chairman Margaret Bush Wilson characterized the *Energy Statement* as the basis to "sound the alarm" about the nation's energy crisis. She cheered Stewart's admonition that the federal government must take a major role to assure its citizens that an energy policy would not restrict vigorous economic growth and thus reduce job opportunities for minorities.[1]

When the NAACP *Energy Statement* was released to members of Congress, some called it "pro-business." Stewart said it was "pro-progress." He defended the policy which called for increased production of domestic oil and natural gas. Stewart told *The Washington Post*, "The statement wasn't pro-industry. . . It was pro-jobs and opportunities for black people for whom it's time to get a piece of the pie. And the only way we're going to get it is if we stimulate industrial growth and exploration and by bringing more energy into the United States. We can't through conservation get any more jobs for blacks."[2]

Oklahoma United States Senator Dewey Bartlett publicly endorsed the policy, asking that it be printed in the *Congressional Record,* and wrote Stewart, thanking him for "great service to our country."[3]

The *Energy Statement* was seen as a major break with the Carter administration by the NAACP. The *Wall Street Journal* called it "a document of major political and social significance," observing that "for the first time in memory the NAACP has sided emphatically with the free-marketers instead of the interventionists on a major question of public policy."[4]

Commentator Paul Harvey, himself a product of oil capital Tulsa, said the NAACP was on target for recommending deregulation of oil and gas and putting more emphasis on nuclear power. Harvey wrote in his syndicated newspaper column, "The NAACP, heretofore concerned mostly with legal barriers to the upward movement of blacks, now recognizes that the barriers to further advancement are mostly economic."[5]

Stewart asked President Carter to consider the findings of his report which expressed fears that employment hardships would fall upon blacks and other minorities if industry was restricted on the amount of energy it could use. The NAACP study predicted that if industrial use of energy was curtailed on the west coast, as many as 350,000 persons, many of them black, would become unemployed within a year.[6]

Stewart was concerned that conservation of energy was not enough to save America from a deepening energy crisis. He wrote, "We must opt for an economy that will create more jobs, not fewer. We must demand a national energy policy which calls for growth and development, rather than the status quo. Conservation simply means carving up the pie so that there are smaller pieces to pass around. We don't want smaller pieces, we want a larger pie!" [7]

Within days of the release of the *Energy Statement*, NAACP Executive Director Hooks was summoned to the White House to discuss energy with President Carter who publicly invited black leaders to make their views on energy known to key members of his administration.

The NAACP *Energy Statement* created a firestorm of reaction from black and white leaders and the nation's press. The *New York Times* said the NAACP had allied itself with the oil industry. The *Washington Post* criticized the NAACP Energy Committee for being stacked with members who worked for utilities. NAACP Board Chairman Margaret Wilson struck back, "Why is it that we can have a legal committee composed entirely of lawyers, a health committee composed entirely of doctors, and we are not supposed to have any energy people on our energy committee?"[8]

Back in Oklahoma City, State Senator E. Melvin Porter demanded that Stewart resign from the NAACP national board of directors and accused Stewart of "doing ONG's bidding under the guise of serving the NAACP." Stewart told a reporter that he was not disturbed to hear Porter's statement because "he's running for office and it's nothing but a publicity stunt."[9]

NAACP Executive Director Hooks lashed out at newspaper and television reporters who questioned the integrity of the Energy Committee, "There is a white elitist assumption that we don't have sense enough to know about things like energy and shouldn't say anything about them."[10]

Even Ronald Reagan, then a nationally-syndicated columnist, and later United States President, got on the bandwagon in support of Stewart's energy policy, "The black leaders understand, as

Stewart was honored in 1980 when the James E. Stewart Industrial Park was dedicated in northeast Oklahoma City. The most important thing in his life, his family, was on hand for the dedication. From left to right: Top row, daughter Zandra, granddaughter Jeania, grandson James Bennett; middle row, Mae Lois, Stewart, grandson James E. Stewart, III; bottom row, granddaughter Shantee, grandson Stacy.

Stewart and his state senator, Vicki Miles-LaGrange, now United States District Judge for the Western District of Oklahoma. The inscription congratulated Stewart on his appointment to the board of Oklahoma Futures, May 6, 1989.

energy gurus don't seem to, that increased economic activity means more jobs and more jobs means denting the stubborn 14 percent unemployment rate among blacks."[11]

Some historians believe that Carter's rebuff of the NAACP *Energy Statement*, and his subsequent handling of the nation's energy crisis, contributed to his defeat at the polls in 1978.

Oklahoma City Northeast, Inc., a government-funded non-profit community group, built a 16,000 square-foot office building at 1500 Northeast Fourth Street in 1980. Stewart had served on the organization's board of directors since its inception in 1974. He was proud when the board voted to name the new building for him. The James E. Stewart Industrial Park was dedicated in June, 1980. The building was the anchor project in a 500-acre industrial park that stretched from Reno and Santa Fe avenues to Northeast Fourth Street and Eastern.

In 1980 Oklahoma City Mayor Patience Latting appointed Stewart to serve as a member of the Northeast Quadrant Plan Study Committee. Governor George Nigh selected Stewart to serve on the Oklahoma State Diamond Jubilee Celebration Committee and on the Governor's Energy Committee.

Stewart was renominated, without opposition, to serve his eighth three-year term on the national board of directors of the NAACP. He attended the National Conference on Energy and Jobs for Minorities sponsored by the National Urban Coalition and helped KOCO-TV in Oklahoma City produce a feature program "Blacks in Oklahoma."

Stewart was a frequent guest on panels at energy symposiums from California to Yale University. He kept busy as ever speaking at NAACP banquets around the nation.

In July, 1982, Stewart was elected chairman of the Oklahoma City Urban Renewal Authority, the same board which he had declared verbal warfare against in the early days of urban renewal. Stewart used the occasion to remind Oklahoma Cityans that the early urban renewal efforts, in his opinion, "wrecked the community, not only the homes, but the little businesses and property and revenue as landlords."[12] Stewart said his very presence on the

URA served as a reminder that minorities are to be considered in future development in northeast Oklahoma City. Stewart's selection as the URA chairman was openly backed by Oklahoma City Mayor Patience Latting and members of the city council.

In 1983 Stewart attended and spoke to the National Conference of Black Mayors and the National Conference of Black Legislators in Washington, D.C. He was inducted into the Afro-American Hall of Fame in Oklahoma City.

In December, 1983, Stewart reluctantly decided to retire as a member of the NAACP national board of directors. He had served faithfully for 27 years. He did not cite his age and health as the reason for not seeking reelection, but said he was troubled by trends on the national board "which are repugnant to my training and principles."[13] Stewart believed that the NAACP was becoming anti-business and was being run by "Harvard, Yale, and Stanford. . . graduates who have barely stuck their feet into the mainstream of American life."[14]

In early 1984, Stewart was appointed by Governor Nigh to serve on the State Narcotics and Controlled Drug Commission. He developed a presentation for the American Petroleum Institute to work toward bringing blacks into the mainstream of American business and industry. Stewart never gave up the fight to level the employment playing field for blacks in Oklahoma City. After retirement, he continued to campaign for the construction of a state employment office in northeast Oklahoma City where, he reasoned, most of the unemployed Oklahoma Cityans lived.

In 1986 Stewart was inducted into the Oklahoma Hall of Fame, the highly prestigious honor sponsored by the Oklahoma Heritage Association. He was presented by his old neighbor, world-famous author Ralph Ellison.

Ellison told a statewide television audience, "As a novelist I often spend a lot of time developing fictional people. I 'make up,' if you will, every aspect of their character and personality. The question that struck me tonight as I thought back over the life of our next honoree was whether I could ever have 'made up' a man like Stewart."[15]

After a videotape reciting Stewart's achievements and reminding viewers that Stewart helped support his widowed mother by searching alleys for rags and bottles, Ellison said, "Not too bad for the little boy who roamed those alleys picking up junk."[16]

A tearful and humble Stewart accepted induction into the Hall of Fame. He thanked his family, his God, and his brothers and sisters who helped him struggle for equality for the masses. He said his selection took him completely by surprise, "They used to call me a communist, now, years later, they honor me."

The following year, the American Association of Blacks in Energy named their annual award for meritorious service in the energy industry the "James E. Stewart Award." Appropriately, Stewart was the first recipient of the award.

Stewart holding a bust of one of his favorite black heroes, Charles Drew. Drew developed blood plasma that saved many lives in World War II. Tragically Drew died of an auto accident in Virginia because segregation prevented his treatment at an all-white hospital. (Courtesy *The Daily Oklahoman*.)

Above top: Stewart, background center, welcomed Enid-born Metropolitan Opera soprano Leona Mitchell and her family to a 1985 celebration at the state capitol where the artist was honored in a joint session of the state legislature.
Immediately above: Mae Lois, Jimmy, and Don Stewart at Jimmy's induction into the Oklahoma Hall of Fame in 1986. (Courtesy *The Daily Oklahoman.*)

Left: From left to right, Bruce Fisher, Sharon Fisher, Hannah Atkins, and Jimmy, February 1991.

Below: Stewart receives a flag flown over the United States Capitol from Sherman Menser, an aide to Oklahoma Congressman Mickey Edwards. In the background is Ben Tipton, popular Oklahoma City radio announcer and city council member. (Courtesy *The Daily Oklahoman*.)

Stewart in his Oklahoma Natural Gas toboggan.

Jimmy and Ma[...] Lois worked vacations into [h]is busy retirement life.

Even into his late seventies, Stewart served on a dozen local boards and commissions. In 1986 he was reappointed to the Bureau of Narcotics and Dangerous Drugs Commission by Governor George Nigh. He regularly spoke about black history to any group that would listen.

When Supreme Court Justice Thurgood Marshall died in 1993, Stewart was interviewed by a newspaper reporter and appeared in a television documentary. Stewart remembered Marshall's answer to a question posed years before in Oklahoma. Someone asked if blacks in Oklahoma had it better than blacks in Mississippi. Marshall's logic was, "Racial discrimination is racial discrimination no matter where it is. If it is wrong in Mississippi, it is wrong in Oklahoma."[17]

In 1994 Stewart was given the Pathmaker Award of the Oklahoma County Historical Society. The Oklahoma City Parks and Recreation Department named a driving range for Stewart on the site of the old fairgrounds at Northeast

Tenth and Martin Luther King, hallowed ground that Stewart fought for, and won, for a new Douglass High School 40 years before. Plans for the golf facility at Douglass Park call for a nine-hole course, to be named the James E. Stewart Golf Course.

Stewart never stopped chiding his fellow blacks where he saw apathy. In 1996 he observed that blacks were less than enthusiastic about celebrating Juneteenth, the June 19 anniversary of the day in 1865 when Texas slaves received word of their freedom as declared by the Emancipation Proclamation. Stewart charged that blacks had become sophisticated and did not properly celebrate what he considered the Fourth of July for blacks. Stewart said, "Some things in history you should never forget."[18]

In 1997 he was chosen for induction into the Oklahoma Journalism Hall of Fame, quite a feat for a part-time journalist who loved sitting at his typewriter in the early morning hours before his regular job, putting the last touches on his weekly column or a special editorial.

Stewart's earthly body, tired from 84 active years of battling for a better Oklahoma and America, passed from this realm April 13, 1997. Hundreds of friends and relatives gathered at the Episcopal Church of the Redeemer on April 18 for a memorial service. ONG Senior Vice President Charles C. Hopper eulogized Stewart

Jimmy and Mae Lois had a quality life...full of love, friendship, and mutual respect and admiration.

as "a manager, a peacemaker and a mainstay of our social conscience." Stewart was buried at Arlington Cemetery. Stewart left behind his wife, Mae Lois, who died a year later.

The Daily Oklahoman paid tribute to Stewart, with these words: "Over decades of work. . . he deftly persuaded white leaders to open doors of opportunity that once were closed to Americans of African descent. . . Stewart's legacy is a lifetime of good work in helping to form a better community and state."[19]

The Black Chronicle said, "Stewart had a consciousness of the need for being conciliatory even while being forceful." The newspaper's publisher, Russell M. Perry, recalled the highlights of Stewart's life. "It was because of men like Stewart that the pain of enduring the ensuing storm with the fall of these walls of evil was made easier. . . made more palatable, if you will. Because of Mr. Stewart's style, we call it, the embitteredness, harsh hatred and divisiveness experienced by many other places having to eliminate segregation was less so in Oklahoma City and in Oklahoma."[20]

Perry wrote, "With this sense of conciliation combined with vigorous, uncompromising advocacy for the elimination of evil, Stewart got things done and we are all better off because of his efforts. The world is a better place because he lived here."[22]

Shortly before his death, Stewart was writing notes for what might have become an autobiography. An excerpt gives a keen insight into his soul and mind:

> Wealth nor power mean much without the knowledge that you
> can go home at night and truly believe that you have done
> harm to no man, nor is any man your enemy. He is rich who
> gives of himself, loves his neighbor, and honors God Almighty.

Jimmy Stewart was a very rich man. Oklahoma, and the nation, will miss him.

NOTES

CHAPTER ONE

1. *Harlow's Weekly* (Oklahoma City), April 1, 1916.

2. *The Black Dispatch* (Oklahoma City), March 5, 1965.

3. *Harlow's Weekly,* April 1, 1916.

4. Ralph Ellison, *Shadow and Act,* (New York: Random House, Inc. 1953), 192.

5. *The Daily Oklahoman* (Oklahoma City), August 4, 1995.

6. *The Black Dispatch,* March 5, 1965.

7. Information from a speech in the files of Jimmy Stewart. The speech is entitled "Brief history of separate schools in Oklahoma City area—1890-1963."

8. *The Black Dispatch,* October 3, 1919.

9. Ada Lois Sipuel Fisher, *A Matter of Black and White,* (Norman: University of Oklahoma Press, 1996)

10. *The Black Dispatch,* February 12, 1931.

11. *Ibid.,* February 4, 1921.

12. *Ibid.,* August 5, 1965.

CHAPTER TWO

1. An exciting account of Charlie Christian and the cultural center on Deep Deuce is found in *Charlie and The Deuce,* by Anita G. Arnold, (Oklahoma City: Black Liberated Arts Center, Inc., 1994)

2. *Saturday Review* (New York, New York), May 17, 1958.

3. William W. Savage, Jr., *Singing Cowboys and All That Jazz,* (Norman: University of Oklahoma Press, 1983), 25-28.

4. *Saturday Review,* July 12, 1958.

5. Savage, *Singing Cowboys and All That Jazz,* 30.

6. *The Black Dispatch,* March 12, 1965.

7. *Ibid.,* August 16, 1952.

8. *Ibid.*

CHAPTER THREE

1. *Gasette* (Oklahoma City), October/November, 1974.

2. Speech, Jimmy Stewart, Black Chronicles Collections, Ralph Ellison Library, Oklahoma City, Oklahoma, Hereinafter cited as BCC.

3. Speech, Jimmy Stewart, BBC.

5. *The Black Dispatch,* September 23, September 30, October 7 and October 14, 1939.

6. *Ibid.,* March 12, 1965.

7. *Ibid.,* July 29, 1939.

CHAPTER FOUR

1. *The Black Dispatch,* February 1, 1957.

2. *Ibid.,* February 8, 1957.

3. Roger Goldman, *Thurgood Marshall, Justice for All,* (New York: Carroll and Graf Publishers, Inc., 1992), 46-48.

4. *The Black Dispatch,* June 17, 1944.

5. Goldman, *Thurgood Marshall, Justice for All,* 48.

6. *Ibid.,* March 30, 1940.

7. *Ibid.,* November 2, 1940.

8. *Ibid.,* June 18, 1940.

9. *Ibid.,* December 30, 1940.

10. *Ibid.*

11. *Ibid.,* May 23, 1942.

12. *Ibid.*

13. *bid.*

14. *Ibid.,* October 10, 1942.

15. *Ibid.*

16. *Ibid.,* March 6, 1943.

17. *Ibid.*

CHAPTER FIVE

1. *Oklahoma City Times* (Oklahoma City), January 10, 1959.

2. "Jimmy Stewart" Archives, Oklahoma Natural Gas Company, Oklahoma City, Oklahoma

3. Jimmie Lewis Franklin, *The Blacks in Oklahoma,* (Norman: University of Oklahoma Press, 1980), 17.

4. Jimmie Lewis Franklin, *Journey Toward Hope,* (Norman: University of Oklahoma Press, 1982), 60.

5. *The Black Dispatch,* April 29, 1937.

6. *Ibid.,* October 30, 1943.

7. *Ibid.,* March 13, 1947.

8. *Ibid.,* April 19, 1947.

9. *Ibid.,* July 17, 1948.

10. *The Daily Oklahoman,* October 17, 1948.

11. *The Black Dispatch,* February 15, 1957.

12. Letter, Jimmy Stewart to Jesse T. Owens, December 13, 1947, BCC.

13. *The Black Dispatch,* September 19, 1947.

14. Radio Script, BCC.

15. *Ibid.*

16. Maxwell W. Balfour to Roger Davis, October 21, 1941, BCC.

17. Ralph E. Luker, *Historical Dictionary of the Civil Rights Movement,* (London: The Scarecrow Press, Inc., 1997), 285-286.

18. *Ibid.,* 288.

CHAPTER SIX

1. George L. Cross, *Blacks in White Colleges,* (Norman: University of Oklahoma Press, 1975), 32.

2. *Missouri ex rel. Gaines v. Canada,* 305 United States 337 (1938)

3. *The Black Dispatch,* March 20, 1948.

4. Ada Lois Sipuel Fisher, *A Matter of Black and White,* (Norman, University of Oklahoma Press, 1996), 105.

5. *Ibid.,* 106.

6. *Ibid.,* 95.

7. *Ibid.*

8. *The Black Dispatch,* January 25, 1946.

9. Fisher, *A Matter of Black and White,* 116.

CHAPTER SEVEN

1. *The Black Dispatch,* September 29, 1951.

2. Mary C. Moon, *Frederick Douglass Moon: A Study of Black Education in Oklahoma,* Ph.D. Dissertation, University of Oklahoma, Norman, 1978, 180-215.

3. *Ibid.*

4. *Ibid.*

5. *Ibid.,* 209.

6. *The Daily Oklahoman,* October 10, 1951.

7. *Oklahoma City Times,* October 18, 1951.

8. *Oklahoma City Times,* November 7, 1951.

9. "Our Challenge," BCC.

10. *Ibid.*

11. *The Black Dispatch,* January 10, 1953.

12. F.D. Moon Papers, Ralph Ellison Library, Oklahoma City, Oklahoma.

13. *The Black Dispatch,* May 7, 1955.

14. *The Daily Oklahoman,* May 2, 1955.

CHAPTER EIGHT

1. Romans 4:21, King James Bible.

2. Interview, Jimmy Stewart, August 13, 1995, BCC.

3. *Ibid.*

4. Jimmy Stewart Speech, no date, BCC.

5. Willie and Mae King to Jimmy Stewart, no date, BCC.

6. *The Black Dispatch,* December 19, 1953.

7. *The Black Dispatch,* November 22, 1952.

8. Interview, Jimmy Stewart, August 13, 1995.

9. Jimmy Stewart to Reverend Virtus Gloe, May 24, 1951, BCC.

10. *1951 Annual Report,*

Oklahoma City Branch, NAACP.

11. *Ibid.*

12. Speech, BCC.

13. *Oklahoma City Advertiser,* April 2, 1952.

14. Martin Luther King, Jr. to Jimmy Stewart, BCC.

15. *The Black Dispatch,* December 19, 1953.

CHAPTER NINE

1. Roy Wilkins to Jimmy Stewart, March 13, 1951, BCC.

2. *The Black Dispatch,* June 28, 1952.

3. *Ibid.*

4. NAACP 43rd Annual Conference Resolutions, BCC.

5. *Ibid.*

6. *The Black Dispatch,* June 28, 1952.

7. *Ibid.*

8. *The Daily Oklahoman,* June 30, 1952.

CHAPTER TEN

1. V.E. McCain to C.R. Smith, March 14, 1952, BCC.

2. Jimmy Stewart to Thurgood Marshall, December 31, 1952, BCC.

3. *Ibid.*

4. *The Black Dispatch,* July 5, 1952.

5. *Ibid.*

6. *Ibid.*

7. Jimmy Stewart to Roscoe Dunjee, August 5, 1953, BCC.

8. *Ibid.*

9. *The Black Dispatch,* December 5, 1953.

10. Speech, Jimmy Stewart, March 15, 1953, BCC.

11. *Ibid.*

12. Interview, Justice Hardy Summers, February 13, 1998, Author's Personal Collection.

13. Jonathan Greenberg, *Staking a Claim, Jake Simmons Jr. and the Making of an African-American Oil Dynasty,* (New York: Atheneum, 1990).

14. Telegrams, BCC.

15. *The Black Dispatch,* January 15, 1955.

16. *Ibid,* January 22, 1955.

CHAPTER ELEVEN

1. *Brown v. Board of Education,* 347 United States 483 (1954); Allan Saxe, *Protest and Reform: The Desegregation of Oklahoma City,* Ph.D. Dissertation, University of Oklahoma, Norman, 1969.

2. Interview with Jimmy Stewart, August 13, 1995, BCC.

3. Press release May 18, 1954, BCC.

4. *Ibid.*

5. *The Black Dispatch,* May 22, 1954.

6. *Brown v. Board of Education of Topeka, Kansas,* 349 United States 294 (1955), commonly referred to as Brown II.

7. Ada Lois Sipuel Fisher, *A Matter of Black and White,* 163.

8. Jimmie Lewis Franklin, *The Blacks in Oklahoma,* (Norman, University of Oklahoma Press, 1980), 54-55.

9. Petition, Oklahoma City Board of Education, June, 1954, BCC.

10. *Ibid.*

11. Jimmy Stewart to Roy Wilkins, March 6, 1955, BCC.

12. Roy Wilkins to Jimmy Stewart, March 9, 1955, BCC.

13. *The Black Dispatch,* February 19, 1955.

14. T.H. McDowell to Reverend Thomas J. Griffin, February 19, 1955, BCC.

15. *The Black Dispatch,* April 23, 1955.

16. *Ibid.*

17. *Ibid.*

18. *Ibid.,* June 11, 1955.

19. *Ibid.,* July 9, 1955.

20. *The Daily Oklahoman,* August 31, 1955.

CHAPTER TWELVE

1. Jimmy Stewart to NAACP members, 1956, BCC.

2. John Hope Franklin, *Race and History,* (Baton Rouge: Louisiana State University Press, 1989), 365.

3. Thurgood Marshall to State Conference Presidents, January 20, 1956, BCC.

4. *New Yorker* Magazine, March 17, 1956, 78-109.

5. *Ibid.*

6. *Ibid.*

7. *Ibid.*

8. *Ibid.*

9. Jay Wilkinson, Bud Wilkinson, *An Intimate Portrait of an American Legend,* (Champagn, Illinois: Sagamore Publishing, 1994), 68-80.

10. Randolph, Wilkins, and Martin Luther King, Jr. to black leaders, April 5, 1957, BCC.

11. *The Black Dispatch,* August 30, 1957.

12. *Ibid.*

13. *Ibid.*

CHAPTER THIRTEEN

1. *Annual Report* of the Oklahoma City Branch, NAACP, January 28, 1958, BCC.

2. *Ibid.*

3. *Ibid.*

4. Clara Luper, *Behold The Walls,* (Oklahoma City: privately printed, no date, 1984), 3.

5. *Ibid., 7.*

6. *Ibid.*

7. Jimmy Stewart to Youth Council, August 19, 1958, BCC.

8. Luper, *Behold The Walls.*

9. *The Daily Oklahoman,* August 23, 1958.

10. *Oklahoma City Times,* September 5, 1958.

11. *Ibid.*

12. *Ibid.*

13. *Ibid.*

14. *Ibid.*

15. Luper, *Behold The Walls,* 25.

16. John Henry Lee Thompson, *The Little Caesar of Civil Rights: Roscoe Dunjee,* Ph.D. Dissertation, Purdue University, Lafayette, Indiana, 1990.

17. *The Black Dispatch,* February 6, 1959.

18. *Oklahoma City Times,* January 10,1959.

19. Luper, *Behold The Walls,* 109.

20. John Henry Lee Thompson, *The Little Caesar of Civil Rights,* 192.

21. *Ibid.,* 196.

22. *The Black Dispatch,* August 5, 1960.

23. *Ibid.,* August 5, 1960.

24. *Ibid.*

25. *Ibid.,* August 19, 1960.

26. Luper, *Behold The Walls,* 162.

27. *Ibid. 165.*

28. *The Daily Oklahoman,* August 24, 1960.

CHAPTER FOURTEEN

1. John Hope Franklin, *Race and History,* 150-151.

2. *The Daily Oklahoman,* August 1, 1962.

3. *Oklahoma City Times,* May 28, 1959.

4. *Ibid.*

5. October 23, 1965 speech, Oklahomans for Progress meeting, BCC.

6. Grant Reynolds to Roy Wilkins, August 7, 1962, BCC.

7. Jimmy Stewart to Roy Wilkins, August 10, 1962, BCC.

8. Henry Bellmon with Pat Bellmon, *The Life and Times of Henry Bellmon,* (Tulsa: Council Oaks Books, 1992), 170.

9. *Ibid.*

10. Thompson, *The Little Caesar of Civil Rights,* 203-204.

11. Report of the Community Relations Commission, July 30, 1963, BBC.

12. *The Daily Oklahoman,* May 7, 1963.

13. *Ibid.,* June 5, 1963.

14. *Ibid.,* June 23, 1963.

15. *Ibid.,* July 6, 1963.

16. Ralph Luker, *Historical Dictionary of the Civil Rights Movement,* (Lanham, Maryland: The Scarecrow Press, 1997), 125.

17. Thompson, *The Little Caesar of Civil Rights,* 205.

18. *Ibid.,* 208-209.

19. Jimmie Lewis Franklin, *The Blacks in Oklahoma,* 61.

CHAPTER FIFTEEN

1. *The Black Dispatch,* March 12, 1965.

2. *Ibid.*

3. Speech, Jimmy Stewart, August 30, 1963, BCC.

4. *Ibid.*

5. *Ibid.*

6. *Ibid.*

7. *Ibid.*

8. Jimmy Stewart Speech to the Oklahoma City Chamber of Commerce, July 31, 1967, BCC.

9. *Ibid.*

10. *Ibid.*

11. *Ibid.*

12. Ralph Luker, *Historial Dictionary of the Civil Rights Movement,* 274-275.

13. *Ibid.,* 257.

14. *Ibid.,* 145.

15. Jimmy Stewart. Speech to Oklahoma City Chamber of Commerce, July 31, 1967.

16. Mike Monroney to Stewart, September 27, 1966.

CHAPTER SIXTEEN

1. Roy Stewart, *Born Grown,* 284.

2. Urban Renewal Authority brochure , Stewart, BBC.

3. *Oklahoma City Times,* June 8, 1966.

4. Roy Stewart, *Born Grown,* 287-288.

5. *The Black Dispatch,* July 8, 1966.

6. *Oklahoma City Times,* June 2, 1966.

7. *Ibid.* June 8, 1966.

8. *The Daily Oklahoman,* June 12, 1966.

9. *The Black Dispatch,* July 8, 1966.

10. *Ibid.*

11. *Ibid.,* June 2, 1966.

12. *Ibid.*

13. *Ibid.,* June 14, 1966.

14. *Ibid.*

15. *Oklahoma Journal*

(Midwest City), June 12, 1966.

16. Jimmy Stewart to City Planning Commission, December 12, 1967, Stewart Collection.

17. *The Daily Oklahoman,* January 4, 1968.

18. *Ibid.,* July 1, 1968.

CHAPTER SEVENTEEN

1. *The Black Dispatch,* September 16, 1960.

2. *Ibid.,* February 24, 1964.

3. *Ibid.,* March 20, 1954.

4. *Ibid.*

5. *Ibid.,* March 20, 1964.

6. *Ibid.*

7. *Ibid.,* February 21, 1964.

8. *Ibid.*

9. *Ibid.,* October 7, 1966.

10. *Ibid.*

11. *Ibid.*

12. *Ibid.,* August 19, 1966.

13. *Ibid.,* June 17, 1966.

14. *Ibid.,* May 17, 1966.

15. *Ibid.,* July 26, 1966.

16. Clara Luper, *Behold The Walls,* 215.

17. *Ibid.,* 216.

18. *Ibid.,* 219.

19. *Ibid.,* 222.

20. Inteview, Reverend W.K. Jackson, January 19, 1998, Archives, Oklahoma Heritage Association, Oklahoma City, Oklahoma.

CHAPTER EIGHTEEN

1. Kenny A. Franks and Paul F. Lambert, *The Legacy of Dean Julian C. Monnet: Judge Luther Bohanon and the Desegreation of Oklahoma City's Public Schools,* (Muskogee: Western Heritage Books, 1984), 11.

2. *Ibid.,* 23-24.

3. *Ibid.,* 29.

4. *Dowell v. Board of Education of the Oklahoma City Public Schools,* 219 F. Supp. 427 (1963).

5. *Dowell v. Board of Education,* 338 F. Supp. 1256, 1972.

6. *The Black Dispatch,* December 2, 1971.

7. Arthur L. Tolson, *The Black Oklahomans,* (New Orleans: Edwards Printing Company, 1975), 200.

8. *Ibid.,* 207.

9. *Ibid..,* 209.

10. *Ibid.,* 208-209.

11. *The Sunday Oklahoman* (Oklahoma City), August 24, 1997.

12. *Ibid.,* August 24, 1997.

13. *Ibid.*

CHAPTER NINETEEN

1. *The Daily Oklahoman,* January 8, 1993.

2. Interview, Judge Jerry Salyer, June 15, 1998, BCC.

3. Villa Savoy Apartments advertising brochure, BCC.

4. *The Black Dispatch,* February 23, 1971.

5. *Ibid.,* January 7, 1971.

6. *Ibid.,* November 18, 1971.

7. *Ibid.,* December 11, 1975.

8. Interview, William N. Pirtle, February 25, 1998, Archives, Oklahoma Heritage Association, Oklahoma City, Oklahoma.

9. Press release, January, 1976, Stewart Collection.

10. Interview, Charles C. Ingram, February 25, 1998, Archives, Oklahoma Heritage Association, Oklahoma City, Oklahoma.

11. *Oklahoman and Times,* September 17, 1977.

12. *Ibid.*

13. *Ibid.*

14. *Ibid.,* August 29, 1977.

15. *Ibid.*

CHAPTER TWENTY

1. *The Crisis* (New York, New York), February, 1980, 41-43.

2. *The Washington Post,* January 12, 1978.

3. Dewey Bartlett to Jimmy Stewart, January 26, 1978, Stewart Collection.

4. *The Wall Street Journal* (New York, New York), January 21, 1978.

5. *The Oklahoma Journal,* February 5, 1978.

6. *Oklahoma City Times,* January 12, 1978.

7. Oklahomans for Energy and Jobs pamphlet, 1978, Stewart Collection.

8. *The Wall Street Journal,* February 7, 1978.

9. *The Oklahoma Journal,* February 2, 1978.

10. *Ibid.*

11. *The Daily Oklahoman,* January 20, 1978.

12. *The Black Chronicle,* June 24, 1982.

13. Jimmy Stewart to M.L. Knotts, August 6, 1982, Stewart Collection.

14. *Ibid.*

15. Introduction speech of Ralph Ellison, 1986 Oklahoma Hall of Fame Awards, Archives, Oklahoma Heritage Association, Oklahoma City, Oklahoma.

16. *Ibid.*

17. *The Daily Oklahoman,* January 28, 1993.

18. *Ibid.,* June 19, 1996.

19. *Ibid.,* April 20, 1997.

20. *Ibid.,* April 20, 1997.

21. *Ibid.*

22. *Ibid.*

BIBLIOGRAPHY

COLLECTIONS

Black Chronicles Collections. Ralph Ellison Library. Oklahoma City, Oklahoma. The collection of the personal papers of Jimmy Stewart to 1977. The remainder of Stewart's papers are held by his family. The incredible collection includes the original, hand-written minute books of the NAACP Oklahoma City Branch, the most authoritative source of much of the history of the civil rights movement in Oklahoma.

Newspaper Archives. Oklahoma Historical Society, Oklahoma City, Oklahoma.

Photographic Collection, *The Daily Oklahoman,* Oklahoma City, Oklahoma.

Jimmy Stewart's Personnel File. Oklahoma Natural Gas Company, Oklahoma City, Oklahoma.

BOOKS

Aldrich, Gene. *Black Heritage of Oklahoma.* Edmond: Thompson Book and Supply Company, 1973.

Arnold, Anita G. *Charlie and The Deuce.* Oklahoma City: Black Liberated Arts Center, Inc., 1994.

Bellmon, Henry with Pat Bellmon. *The Life and Times of Henry Bellmon.* Tulsa: Council Oak Books, 1992.

Burke, Bob and Angela Monson. *Roscoe Dunjee: Champion of Civil Rights.* Edmond: University of Central Oklahoma Press, 1998.

_____ and Kenny A. Franks. *Dewey Bartlett: The Bartlett Legacy.* Edmond: University of Central Oklahoma Press, 1996.

Creel, Von Russell and Bob Burke. *Mike Monroney: Oklahoma Liberal.* Edmond: University of Central Oklahoma Press, 1997.

Cross, George L. *Blacks in White Colleges.* Norman: University of Oklahoma Press, 1975.

Ellison, Ralph. *Shadow and Act.* New York: Random House, Inc., 1953.

Fisher, Ada Lois Sipuel. *A Matter of Black and White.* Norman: University of

Oklahoma Press, 1996.

Franklin, Jimmie Lewis. *The Blacks in Oklahoma.* Norman: University of Oklahoma Press, 1980.

_____. *Journey Toward Hope.* Norman: University of OklahomaPress, 1982.

Franklin, John Hope. *Race and History.* Baton Rouge: Louisiana State University Press, 1989.

Franks, Kenny A. and Paul F. Lambert. *The Legacy of Dean Julian C. Monnet: Judge Luther Bohanon and the Desegregation of Oklahoma City's Public Schools.* Muskogee: Western Heritage Books, 1984.

Goldman, Roger. *Thurgood Marshall-Justice for All.* New York: Carroll and Graf Publishers, Inc., 1992.

Greenberg, Jack. *Crusaders in the Courts.* New York: Basic Books, 1994.

Harris, Jacqueline L. *History and Achievement of the NAACP.* New York: The African-American Experience, 1992.

Luker, Ralph. *Historical Dictionary of the Civil Rights Movement.* Lanham,

Maryland: The Scarecrow Press, 1997.

Luper, Clara. *Behold The Walls*. Oklahoma City: privately printed, 1984.

Milligan, James C. and L. David Norris. *Raymond D. Gary: The Man on The Second Floor*. Muskogee: Western Heritage Books, 1988.

McKissack, Patricia and Fredrick. *The Civil Rights Movement in America from 1865 to Present*. Chicago: Childrens' Press, 1990.

Savage, William W. Jr. *Singing Cowboys and All That Jazz*. Norman: University of Oklahoma Press, 1983.

Shirley, Glenn. *Law West of Fort Smith*. New York: Henry Holt and Company, 1957.

Stewart, Roy P. *Born Grown*. Oklahoma City: Fidelity Bank, 1984.

Teall, Kaye M. *Black History in Oklahoma-A Resource Book*. Oklahoma City: Oklahoma City Public Schools, 1971

Tolson, Arthur L. *The Black Oklahomans*. New Orleans: Edwards Printing Company, 1975.

Wilkinson, Jay. *Bud Wilkinson, An Intimate Portrait of an American Legend*. Champagn, Illinois: Sagamore Publishing, 1994.

NEWSPAPERS

Gassette, Oklahoma City, Oklahoma.

Harlow's Weekly, Oklahoma City, Oklahoma.

New York Times, New York, New York.

Oklahoma City Advertiser, Oklahoma City, Oklahoma.

Oklahoma City Times, Oklahoma City, Oklahoma.

Oklahoma Journal, Midwest City, Oklahoma.

The Daily Oklahoman, Oklahoma City, Oklahoma.

The Sunday Oklahoman, Oklahoma City, Oklahoma.

The Black Chronicle, Oklahoma City, Oklahoma.

The Black Dispatch, Oklahoma City, Oklahoma.

Washington Post, Washington, D.C.

PERIODICALS

New Yorker, New York, New York.

Saturday Review, New York, New York.

The Crisis, New York, New York.

UNPUBLISHED DISSERTATIONS

Hadley, Worth J. Roscoe Dunjee on Education: The Improvement of Black Education in Oklahoma, 1930-1955. University of Oklahoma, Norman, 1981.

Hubbell, John T. Racial "Desegregation at the University of Oklahoma, 1946-1950." University of Oklahoma, Norman, 1961.

Moon, Mary C. "Frederick Douglass Moon: A Study of Black Education in Oklahoma." University of Oklahoma, Norman, 1978.

Saxe, Allan. "Protest and Reform: The Desegregation of Oklahoma City," University of Oklahoma, Norman, 1969.

Spears, Earnestine Beatrice. "Social Forces in the Admittance of Negroes to the University of Oklahoma." University of Oklahoma, Norman, 1951.

Thompson, John Henry Lee. "The Little Caesar of Civil Rights: Roscoe Dunjee." Purdue University, Lafayette, Indiana, 1990.

INDEX